Cleaning

Cleaning

— ❖ —

SAHAJ MARG
EDUCATIONAL SERIES
Volume 2

Compiled by Ferdinand Wulliemier
Sahaj Marg Research Institute

SHRI RAM CHANDRA MISSION

Shri Ram Chandra Mission
Post Office Box 269
Molena, GA 30258
U.S.A.

http://www.srcm.org

First Edition: February, 1998

Printed in United States of America

06 05 04 03 02 01 00 99 98   8 7 6 5 4 3 2 1

ISBN 0-945242-38-7

Contents

Preface

*I have to finally give another talk on cleaning, maybe, because
it's the most important thing in Sahaj Marg.*

Chariji

In the first volume of the Sahaj Marg Educational Series, titled
Meditation, we explained the reasons for compiling these texts,
their classification and the way we have proceeded for their pres-
entation.

The same procedure has been used and the same Sahaj Marg
books are reviewed in this text on cleaning, with the addition of
Letters of the Master, vol. III, and the last two *Principles of Sahaj
Marg* (vol. IX and X) which were not yet printed when *Meditation* was produced. *Autobiography Of Ram Chandra*, volumes I
and II, have been replaced as references by *Complete Works of
Ram Chandra*, volume III, which also contains *Messages Universal*. No pertinent quotations were found in *India in the West* and
Religion & Spirituality A total of thirty-nine books have been
used for the present compilation.

For the sake of clarification we have also included a short
section entitled "What Cleaning is Not", so that cleaning is dis-
cerned from cleanliness, transmission and meditation. The pas-
sages related to the concept of purification have been considered
as synonyms of our Sahaj Marg cleaning procedure and quoted as
such.

We do hope that the attentive reading of this second volume of
our Sahaj Marg Educational Series and the full practice of it will
be very useful to all abhyasis of Shri Ram Chandra Mission in
contributing to our spiritual evolution. This will enable us to derive complete benefit from the next volume, entitled *Love,* to be

published in the Jubilee year 1999, both title and publishing date decided by our President and living Master, Shri Parthasarathi Rajagopalachari.

Along this line, let us end this preface with an illustrative quote of Chariji's: "The primary thing for us is therefore to make ourselves empty, so that the bowl may be filled up with the Master's Grace."

Ferdinand Wulliemier
Switzerland
September 1997

Acknowledgements

The present text have been published with the help of the following dedicated workers:

Marie-Laure Bodet

Tom Nyland Hansen

Lucie Hautefeuille

Jennifer Henchoz

Christine Prisland

Nicole Renevey

Sydnie Steinberg

Martine Van Overloop

Diana Waycott

George Zogbi

Lalaji
Shri Ram Chandraji of Fatehgarh, U.P.
Adi-Guru, Shri Ram Chandra Mission

Babuji
Shri Ram Chandraji of Shahjahanpur, U.P.
Founder-President, Shri Ram Chandra Mission

Chariji
Shri Parthasarathi Rajagopalachariji
President, Shri Ram Chandra Mission

"Without cleaning you'll not get anywhere."

Shri P. Rajagopalachari

PART ONE

— ❖ —

WHAT CLEANING IS NOT

CLEANLINESS

Here we feel glimpses of soul and our experiences at the point are of similar nature. For this reason it is known as the seat of *atman*. Cleanliness and simplicity are the characteristic features of this state. (*Complete Works of Ram Chandra*, vol. I, p. 259)

It has been said for ages that cleanliness is next to godliness, but it is a commentary on human understanding that, as with everything else, we have given a very superficial interpretation to this statement. Through generations of human life, we find that civilizations have concentrated exclusively on the physical cleanliness of our living conditions. And in most nations of the world, we have made considerable progress in this direction, although in countries like mine, and all over the East, we are still living under very dirty living conditions. At least the impression of the Easterner when he comes to the West is one of absolute cleanliness, and when the Westerner goes to the East it is the contrary opinion of absolute filth. Superficially, these personal impressions or opinions are correct. In my travels though Europe during the last twenty-five years, I have found that conditions of cleanliness have been increasing day by day, year by year, till today in the very advanced nations of the world, the cleanliness inside the house is almost clinically sterile. Of course much effort goes into maintaining it that way.

There is a surprising comment I have heard often that in the East we employ a lot of servants to keep our houses clean. I have often tried to explain that when we use vacuum cleaners, detergents, electric appliances for cooking etc., the energy that we use is nothing but the consolidation of the services of a vast army of servants. Now the use of servants, human servants, has some definite advantages. First it provides employment for people who badly need it and, secondly and more importantly, it does not pollute the atmosphere and our surroundings. The most important advantage is the conservation of scarce energy resources. But of course human effort can only be limited to the number of people available for service. So we find a peculiar inversion that in the eastern countries there is a lot of dirt around our life but we do not have pollution of our rivers, of our lakes, of our atmosphere, while here in the West we have clinical conditions of life inside the house, whereas in the lakes and the seas the fish are unable to live, and a stage is slowly coming when we will be unable to breathe the atmosphere we live in. I have not talked about cleanliness to make criticism of our ways of life, either of yours or of mine, I have tried to show you that when there is no balance between the outside and the inside, something has to suffer in consequence.

So far I have talked to you about the outside and the inside of our homes. There is a more important association of two sides within the human system itself. As we have an outside, we also have an inside which is within us. Here again, there is a big hiatus between the people of the East and the people of the West. My Master has often remarked that in the East, where people are so dirty outside, they seem to have an inner spiritual cleanliness which seems to be lacking in people of the advanced nations who are very clean outside but have a lot of grossness inside. I have deliberately used the word grossness because grossness is not uncleanliness *per se*. Now it is this inner grossness that is a bar to our advancement on the spiritual path. Hitherto, this subject of inner cleanliness has been largely neglected. Even advanced yogic systems, such as the hatha yoga and other systems, have restricted their efforts more to the perfection of the physical system than to the perfection of the inner life of man. I think it is one of the unique features of my Master's system of Sahaj Marg that the greatest importance is given to the cleaning of the inner system, the spiritual system, of man.

(*Principles of Sahaj Marg,* vol. I, p.106-108)

TRANSMISSION

... I gave you that example, you know — cleaning can never cause harm, so it's for your good. And all the lightness that you feel during a sitting is not due to transmission at all, it's due to cleaning. Cleaning gives you lightness. Transmission, when you are light, gives you the feeling of going deep into the meditation. Transmission, when it is gross, produces vibrations, all these funny things, you see. The subtler it is, the more you must feel that there has been nothing happening in the meditation. But after the sitting is over you feel the difference. These are some things we should know, you see.   (*Preceptor's Guide*, vol. I, p. 265)

— ❖ —

A very common misconception is that cleaning is effected by transmission. If one reads through Master's instructions, he says, "Transmit for a few minutes, and try to read the condition of the abhyasi. Do this for four or five minutes. Then clean thoroughly. Then transmit again for a few minutes and read the condition again. If the cleaning is over, then transmit for the rest of the sitting." What is used in cleaning the abhyasi? It is the will power of the preceptor. Transmission is stopped when the cleaning is being done. Otherwise would not the transmission itself serve to exaggerate the latent tendencies of the individual?

(Preceptor's Guide, vol. II, p. 299)

MEDITATION

You see, here comes the need for faith, confidence, and the application of will power. I think in Courmettes I had a discussion about meditation and cleaning, what is the basic difference. The basic difference is that in meditation your mind is brought to a state of passivity applied to a single object to promote or develop concentration, and there it rests. There is no question of will power during meditation. In cleaning there is no meditation, there is only the application of will power used to remove grossness, impurities, complexes, progressively, stage by stage, initially upon the whole heart when you don't have the capacity to read. (*Preceptor's Guide*, vol. II, p.125)

In meditation we don't apply our will at all. In meditation it's a question of fixing our attention on the object on which we are meditating. Now this is perhaps why many people find that instead of doing the cleaning they're meditating, because if the will is not applied, it becomes something of a farce. But because we sit in the aspect of meditation, in the attitude, or in the posture we normally adopt, the mind having become used to meditation, it slips into meditation. (*Fruit of the Tree*, p. 9)

PART TWO

— ❖ —

WHAT CLEANING IS

Truth Eternal
Shri Ram Chandraji of Fatehgarh U.P.

He used to transmit, cleanse and transform them saying that his work was that of a sweeper or washerman. Whoever came to him would be cleansed through and through. After his Manas was cleaned he would get a guide according to his *samskaras*.   (p. 10)

The soul of a human being will be clean in proportion to the power of discrimination he possesses.   (p. 15)

Cleanse your Manas (mind) with practice of Sadhana and then go through literature, otherwise Reality will be lost upon you.
(p.16)

Complete Works of Ram Chandra, Volume I
Shri Ram Chandra

Spiritual training starts with inner cleaning or the purification of 'Chakras' which is the most essential factor in spiritual advancement. Thus the right type of training in spirituality, begins with inner cleaning which, if neglected, will lead to abuse of power acquired through Yogic means. Hatha Yoga lays down mostly physical practices to effect cleaning, some of which are too hard and tedious for all and sundry, while under the system of

'Sahaj Marg' it is accomplished by easy mental practices, aided by the power transmitted by the teacher.   (p.67)

Strenuous labour with long and tedious physical practices as commonly recommended by teachers in order to effect the moulding of mind or the cleaning of the Chakras, is consequently not of much avail. For this purpose we utilize our thought power in a proper way, under the guidance of a powerful Master who is capable of removing complexities and entanglements that hinder our progress and who transmits into us the force necessary for the upkeep of our spiritual life.   (p.67)

The right course of training for an aspirant of spirituality, therefore, is to proceed along the path of realization under the guidance of a true and worthy master in the most natural way, with due regard to inner cleanliness or purification of Chakras and complete moderation in the exercise of the senses and other faculties.   (p.73)

The feeling of *Vairagya* in the real sense and with the lasting results can only be developed after thorough cleaning and due moderation.   (p.98)

The next higher in rank and position is a Dhruva. He enjoys mastery over *Brahmanda Mandal* and falls under the category of Muni. His sphere of work is much larger and he exercises authority over the Vasus. His duty is to look to the cleaning of the atmosphere of all unwanted thoughts and ideas prevailing within. Besides his routine work he has also to look to numerous other duties entrusted to him for the time being.   (p.105)

Thus our attention being directed towards the attainment of purity of that highest level, we began to imitate it in all outward ways, looking particularly to the cleaning of the body. The external ways adopted for the purpose began to cast their effect upon the mind and thus the internal purity too began to develop. This continued process supplemented by our firm attention upon the Ideal contributed greatly to the attainment of the highest purity. The process thus being accelerated, real purity began to flow in all through, and the mind began to get purified, producing good thoughts which helped us further in our pursuit.   (p.200)

In the evening again sit in the same posture, at least for half an hour and think that the complexities, the network of your previous thoughts and grossness or solidity in your constitution are all melting away, or evaporating in the form of smoke, from your back. It will help you in purging your mind and will make you receptive of the efficacious influence of our great Master. As soon as I find that you are free from foreign matter I will either change it in some other way or ask you to stop, as the case may be. In this way, we soar up high by awakening and cleaning the chakras and the sub-points thereof, taking up *kundalini* at the end, with which the abhyasi has nothing to do himself. It is exclusively the outlook of the Master. But it must be remembered that while practising these methods one should not force his mind too much but only sit in a normal way. This process of cleaning is to be repeated for about five minutes before meditational practice in the morning as well. Other ways of cleaning may also be advised according to the needs of individual abhyasis, and need not be mentioned here in detail. Suffice it to say, that the process of cleaning uses the original power of thought in the form of human will for the refinement of the individual soul to enable it to ascend the steep and slippery path of realisation of the subtlest Essence of Identity.   (p.342-343)

Complete Works of Ram Chandra, Volume II
Shri Ram Chandra

... the attainment of the other, i.e., 'pain' is not of course any
child's play. The greatest saints have passed away, ever thirsting
for it. A good many of them must have tasted 'peace' but let us
now have a taste of that for a spark of which one might well
forego a thousand states of peace and calmness. This is the foundation of the structure which helps to bring forth rare personalities into the world. I may also say that that is perhaps the best
way of serving humanity, and a pursuer of this path cannot but be
successful. It helps immensely the unfolding of the knots to clear
the abhyasi's way onwards.   (p.4)

During my leisure hours I remain mostly busy with cleaning
the abhyasis under my training, in order to develop in them the
remembrance of God all through, and this service is for me a
substitute for God's worship, hence my foremost duty. But that is
a very tedious job and requires quite a long time which might
perhaps exhaust the patience of the abhyasi. As a general rule one
does not feel much interested in meditation when the cleaning
process is being effected, or when impressions and bondages are
being loosened, which is in fact the only effective course and one
greatly helpful to his sacred cause.   (p.11)

⚓ None in the world is free from worries. The presence of af-
flictions is in fact a positive proof of the very existence of man.
Worries are really the result of the unbalanced activity which had
originally brought man into existence. This is the inter-play of the
forces of Nature, causing expansions and contractions, by the
effect of which layer after layer began to be formed. Now if one
keeps his entire attention located on them thinking that thereby he
may minimise their effect, it is almost impossible. Ages may be

lost in the pursuit, not to speak of this one life; on the other hand, he will go on fabricating greater intricacies by his own actions. That is really the misutilisation of the powers bestowed on us by Nature. If we keep ourselves concerned with the clearing off of the limitations set up by the expansion and contraction of the forces, our purpose may be rightly served. It is therefore necessary for us to start from the level where Nature's forces begin to promote consciousness in man. The reason why people are not able to undertake it is that they do not attach any importance to it, because they have no definite aim or purpose in view. An archer can never hit at the mark unless he fixes his keen attention on the object to be hit.

I have my own experiences of sufferings and miseries, and after pondering over them a good deal I have now come to the conclusion that suffering and disease are the boons of Nature in disguise which helps deliverance from the effects of *samskaras*. When one is cleared of their remnants, spiritual progress goes on unabated, provided one's mind is inwardly inclined towards it.

(p.32-33)

In the evening sit again in the same easy posture for half an hour and think that the complexities, the network of your previous thoughts and grossness or solidity in your body, are all melting away or evaporating in the form of smoke from your back side. It will help you in purging your mind and make you receptive of the efficacious influence of our great Master. As soon as I find that you are free from undesirable matter I will take appropriate action. We soar high by awakening and cleaning the chakras and the sub-points thereof, taking up *kundalini* also in the end, with which the abhyasi has nothing to do by himself.   (p.67)

⟡ I am glad that you are eager to reach the stage of *vairagya*. You will attain it without doubt, but only when you are sufficiently cleaned; and it depends upon you as well, for which you are advised the evening practice. I feel you are improving spiritually, for which I give you a hint to understand. You must be feeling lightness, though only a little, which is a sign that complexities are melting away gradually and the spiritual force is flowing into you. Try to feel it and inform me accordingly. If you do not get time for meditation during the day then do it when you go to bed, or after midnight (after a short sleep) when everything around is calm and quiet. In that case proceed first with the cleaning process fixed for the evening. Do it for about fifteen minutes and after it devote an hour or so to meditation as directed.   (p.69-70)

⁰ God alone is in fact the real guide or guru, and we all get light from Him alone. But only he who has cleaned his heart to that extent feels it coming therefrom, while a common man engrossed deeply in material complexities feels it not. He therefore stands in need of one of his fellow beings of high calibre to help him in that direction. We may call him guide, guru, master or by whatever name we like, but he is after all a helper and a supporter, working in the spirit of service and sacrifice. His role is by far the most important, for it is he who, as a matter of fact, pulls the real seeker up and enlivens him with the light which is lying in him under layers of grossness. The light thus awakened begins first to cast its reflection upon outer coverings and removes grossness and impurities therefrom. By and by it goes on developing, affecting the deeper layers also. The light can, however, be awakened by independent efforts as well, but that requires persistent labour for many years together. For this reason association with a worthy guide is of immense value to the abhyasi, since the Master too, in duty bound, keeps on removing obstructions and impediments on the path.   (p.88)

A capable Master, by applying his power through transmission, diverts the tendencies of the abhyasi's mind upwards, with the result that they begin to get moulded and grow comparatively calm and peaceful. He also gives to the abhyasi's *pind*-mind (material-particularised consciousness) a dip into the condition of the *brahmanda*-mind (subtler or cosmic consciousness), after effecting its proper cleaning. The process accelerates the abhyasi's flight towards higher regions. (p.97)

● I did not take in any one but my Master, nor did I ever look to any other but him. It is, as a general rule, the primary duty of a true disciple and the only key to success. That is the only means which helps the removing of impurities from the heart and the overcoming of all obstructions on the path. It effects the unfoldment of the knots. It is in fact the real essence of all *sadhanas*. (p.195)

Under the system of Sahaj Marg the dormant energies of the Centre and sub-centres are awakened so as to enable them to function properly. When the higher centres are awakened they begin to shed their effect upon the lower centres, and when they come into contact with the Divine, the lower ones get merged in them. The higher centres thus take over charge of the lower ones. The lower centres too are cleaned so as to relieve them of the grosser effects settled on them. That alone is the proper, and the most natural, course which can bring about the highest results. (p.212)

There are plexuses, centres and sub-centres which also bar our progress at earlier stages. We have to pass through these in our pursuit of Reality. Complications also arise by the effect of our

wrong thinking and practice, which we have to clear off through
the process of cleaning.   (p.218)

Under this system much emphasis is laid on removing the
grossness so that the overcloudyness which hovers around the
soul be removed. That is for all preceptors of the Mission an important part of their duty. Still much is to be done in this respect
by the abhyasi himself, who is prescribed a method for the purpose.   (p.257)

When the higher centres are awakened, they begin to shed
their effect upon the lower centres, and when they come in contact with the Divine, the lower ones get merged into them.

Thus the higher centres take over charge of the lower ones.
The lower centres too are cleaned so as to relieve them of the
grosser effect which keeps them enwrapped.   (p.259)

❡ The Master attends to the cleaning of the system by removing
mal (grossness), *vikshep* (fickleness) and *avaran* (coverings) and
is a great help to the abhyasi throughout his spiritual career.

We have come down from the main source, and when we want
to return there we will have to ascend, crossing the different
chakras or plexuses. I am not dealing here with the technique of
Sahaj Marg, but with a few things necessary for those who have
formed their tendency to rise above themselves. The training
under Sahaj Marg starts from *karan sharir* (causal body) where
the impressions are in seedling form. We do not stop the thoughts
which come to the abhyasi but we try to clean every centre of the
nerves and the mind lake (chit-lake) itself. We clean the very
bottom of the mind lake from where the waves start. If we somehow succeed in stopping its waves, the matter which gives them

rise will remain as it is. It is possible that by the force of the will the thought waves may be stopped, but the matter which had given rise to those thought waves remains. And if it is not removed, the liberation is not possible. We should proceed in a natural way so that the poison at the root may be removed. Our associates also complain of the incursions of the thoughts, but they are happy at the same time since they find thoughts less disturbing. (p.267)

ℓ The thoughts, which the mind creates, help a great deal to bring the past impressions to *bhoga*. Some people may be afraid that, if they adopt the yogic means and the trail of samskaras continues, they may be in greater difficulties and may suffer from ailments, diseases and accidents. They may be right in their fears. But if such a thing is to happen the presence of the Master will, in that case, become useless. The abhyasi himself works in removing their intensity, and the force of the Master too helps the abhyasi in his efforts to fry them to a great extent. The method may look foreign to the readers, but it is the ancient method which lay buried so far. The effect of the *bhoga* is not so serious as the abhyasi considers, in spite of the fact that so many impressions have pushed themselves for the *bhoga*. The cleaning of the system itself means the removing of all these things. The cleaning of the system brings the desired result very soon, and we become lighter and *sookshma* day by day to secure union with the Lightest. (p.268)

* As long as we do not remove the grossness settled in our centres, the grace or effect of higher centres remains far apart due to the grossness and complexities we have made. Our Sahaj Marg recommends the method for the cleaning of the centres, and the Master himself does it through the process of transmission. (p.277)

Now when this very energy got concentrated, it came to be called as solid, or matter, due to the force of the action. Now you have to remove this very solidity from the abhyasi, so that he may become spirit from top to toe.   (p.318)

It has also come to my experience that God takes over some of the responsibility upon Himself even before the completion of the training. But when he takes over full charge of the abhyasi, the Master's work is practically over, though he has yet to go on with cleaning, if needed, in order to smoothen Nature's work. (p.328)

Why do we meditate on the heart when the brain alone thinks of everything? The heart is the field of work for the mind, and all the points which are in the body and the brain, almost all of them, are found in the heart and, by meditating on it, it facilitates in purifying all those points.   (p.363)

You have written that the worldly worries create heaviness in the heart. This proves that the heart is purified to such an extent that even the sweet fragrance of the flower cannot be endured by it. Nevertheless, the worries should be in the flying form so that the heart may not be aware of them.   (p.363)

Western philosophy is based on doubt, whereas it has no place in Eastern philosophy. To harbour doubt is to give room for a thief in the house. Brother, all these things will be known from practice (abhyas) automatically. The method must be correct and the guide an adept. One should remove grossness and go on dwelling in subtler conditions.   (p.371)

Now, our actions went against the Nature and created a mess in the environment, whereby our own throats are being cut. These things now require to be cleaned, which is being done to a certain extent and will be continued. It has all to be done by you people only, and unknowingly every saint does something. (p.371)

— ❖ —

It is seen that people do not get benefit from the evening practice of cleaning. The reason is that they do it in a faulty way. Inform all the persons conducting satsangh under your centre and explain orally to whomsoever you meet. In fact, people first begin to meditate on grossness, and then think that it is going from the back side in the form of smoke. Really speaking, they ought to throw it out by thought-suggestion, in the form of smoke.

(p.372)

— ❖ —

It happens that sometimes during meditation the abhyasi feels absorbed, while sometimes he does not. The reason is that the samskaras which are firmly rooted in their 'field' come towards the heart to go out. This is because meditation creates a vacuum in the heart. As long as all samskaras are not thrown out, there cannot be Liberation. As a matter of fact I go on cleaning them in the routine course also. (p.375)

 Complete Works of Ram Chandra, Volume III
Shri Ram Chandra

For this, in our Sahaj Marg system, methods of cleaning are also given and the Master laid stress on it. Dr. K.C. Varadachari of Tirupati, has said somewhere that the cleaning system is found nowhere except in grains in Jainism. (p.22)

Lalaji told me that cleaning is necessary for all, and that all those who had received training from him had spoiled themselves by accumulating grossness in themselves. I was asked to clean them.					(p.164)

Lalaji told me that he used to clean the evil effects intended to be produced in me during sleep.					(p.165)

Hadees-e-nafs is that condition where one entangles oneself in the net like a spider. The thread will not break unless a jerk is given. The means to save oneself from it is that as soon as this condition makes its appearance, one should merge himself in thought; i.e., that thought which pervades everything in life. The method of cleaning it is that the threads of all these should be broken.					(p.192)

The condition is called 'living dead'. This is *jeevan-mukti* in the real sense, provided that the condition of the dead is really produced. The real thing is beyond this. I (Lalaji) had this condition from my birth. And dear Ram Chandra, too, inherits the same.

Question: How can this condition be acquired?

Answer: I will show the practice in a nutshell. One should go on cleaning his temperament (tendency) which is generally exhibited outwardly. It will help in attaining this condition.					(p.230)

ʼ Now, the need of the time is that the lower centres should also be taken up side by side. No doubt, you have at some places taken the lowest points for cleaning. From today I advise that after cleaning the heart, the *pinda* also should be cleaned. Afterwards, the transmission should be continued from the heart as you are doing at present. (p.250)

Swami Vivekananda stressed the importance of the cleaning process so that the defects may not be further strengthened by the power of Reality. That is to say, cleaning is important so that the Reality may not give power to those filthy things. (p.285)

There are plexuses, centres and sub-centres which also bar our progress at earlier stages. We have to pass through these in our pursuit of Reality. Complications also arise by the effect of our wrong thinking and practice, which we have to clear off through the process of cleaning. (p.369)

— ❖ —

By the prayer, we go from outside noise to outside silence. By cleaning, we go from outside silence to inside silence. (p.411)

Letters of the Master, Volume I - 1954 to 1959
[Letters between Babuji and Dr. K.C. Varadachari]

The meditation I have written to you is not to gain anything so that you may develop idolatory but it is for the cleaning of the different forms of idolatory which have entered into being. (p.61)

With all the respect to the sage I cannot help saying that the idea of cleaning the system prevails only in your *sanstha*. It is of course a very tedious job but it has grown into mania to me. (p.104)

☞ Master so far as I know I tried to read the internal conditions. Sometimes I am successful after five or ten minutes. In the meanwhile my absorption in myself comes up and then again I revert to my work of cleaning the abhyasi. They do not feel anything except improvement and calm, (p.225)

I hope Appaji must be feeling calm as you have done his spiritual service. I must tell you one thing about it that the outer surface of the heart is quite clean, but there is grossness in the inner layers, for which please be attentive. Please take the cleaning of the whole system which includes *sookshma* body. I will also help you in this matter. (p.277)

Sometimes I was able to see the condition of the abhyasi clearly and was cleaning the system. Sometimes I was able only to intuit or I was somehow suggested the condition of the abhyasi. Sometimes I somehow hazarded the description of the abhyasi's condition, which the abhyasis confirmed. (p.326-327)

On the night of December 25, while I was transmitting to you on the point E, I found you to be moving in the central region. I, of course went with you to ensure your safe arrival. This was due to your unconscious devotion and the thorough cleaning of your system. (p.331)

☀ As I wrote to you, I am keeping Chi. Narayana here itself for a year more for advanced work and then make him get into a College as Lecturer. Maybe the forces here may be changed by Thy Grace for it is one of my desires and ambitions that Shri

Venkatesvara University and Tirupati itself and the shrine have to be thoroughly cleaned and purified so that the Centre may be the finest in South India. I am even here sure that my humble wish will find approval from the Master and it will be done soon. More and more it has become clear to me that cleaning of the Indian soul from within is absolutely necessary and urgent and that Master's method of transmission will bring out quick and immediate results in the souls of the people.   (p.363)

Letters of the Master, Volume II - 1960 to 1971
[Letters between Babuji and Dr. K.C. Varadachari]

There is every hope for the betterment of India and the world at large. The personality working for the change of the world has almost finished his work, and it is coming very slowly to the earth in material form because if it is brought into full swing, the personality will have to depart immediately as his work will be over. I think I have mentioned it in my previous letter also. You have done well to exert yourself in cleaning the planets just like our world, they also have become charged with heaviness and grossness. The cleaning of the celestial worlds too is essential since the overhauling of the entire Universe is imminent and destined.   (p.66)

I recall the *anubhav* of Dr. Kuppuswamy about myself when he saw me infusing divine influence in the Universe. May I ask you if you feel the same thing in cleaning the atmosphere, which has grown poisonous. The work is automatic. If you do not feel please lie down on the cot quietly and see that the work is carried on. I want to open this condition a little more.   (p.74)

It sometimes happens even with advanced *sadhakas* that souls appear in order to partake of the effect coming to them from the Master. This happened to me several times during my abhyas period. Souls from even other worlds sometimes come down for this purpose. I had one such case of Chandra Lok and one of Surya Lok. Besides, I am sometimes drawn to other worlds for the purpose. I am sure the soul appearing to you was one from Chandra Lok. I now like to say that you should in your leisure hours transmit to her after due cleaning. (p.98)

 A new condition revealed in you by the direct touch of Almighty. I cannot even touch that point. In this way my task is over. In your case I am only guided to take you to a fresh ring when the former is complete. No transmission is necessary and no cleaning is required except to keep you guarded by the forces of the thoughts swimming in the atmosphere to avoid disturbance in your present condition, which is developing. (p.175)

Silence of course counts much in developing the power of speech but it is better to try for the inner silence so that the words and actions may become charged with the silent force, and that is the spiritual stage which comes in the long run. When this spiritual stage comes in, the impressions of the past almost die and the divine impressions take their place. For this purpose cleaning of every nerve centre is essential, which I hope you will please take note of. (p.262)

It is about a week I am having an idea that the atmosphere, polluted due to evil thoughts of the people, be purged out of poisonous effect thoroughly. There is one person somewhere in India doing the work. Still I need one more man. Can you suggest one?

I have chosen Seshadri for some other work. He can be given this work also but it will be boring for him. Raghavendra Rao (Raichur) has already been given a duty of some other work. But I have not brought them up to the Divine post. For the work of cleaning of atmosphere one must be at *dhruvagati*.   (p.351)

— ❖ —

 As an example, in your case, I feel an imaginary cord from *kantha chakra* to *nabhi*. In it God's work is there. But it is throwing out something and that is being removed by one. My eyes are so trained that I do not want to see anything awkward in our abhyasis and with that idea I am working. Suppose I do not work, where will it go from the system? At this stage cleaning is not very necessary because actually there is no grossness but only a reflection of it which requires attention.   (p.358)

Letters of the Master, Volume III -1966 to 1972
[Letters between Babuji and P. Rajagopalachari]

 But the sound comes when we clap both the hands. If we think of the heart in three layers, we will find that in the frontal layer there is surface tension. On the second layer just after it there is light. The third and the last is dark. In spite of all this there is some slight spiritual intoxication due to initiation. I entrust you with this duty of cleaning not only that but the whole of *Pind Pradesh*, and then write to me about these things.   (p.77)

— ❖ —

I eagerly wish that you get sanction of your leave and be here with me for some time. If you come I will be able to know verbally the effect of my work. If somehow you are not coming then please write to me after a week.

I assure you, I want Bahu (Sulochana) may rise spiritually very high. I asked you to clean the heart and *atma* plexus around which there is an imaginary circle, which, in a way, has made the heart and the *atma* chakra interned. I have just tried to know her past life so that I may proceed through the base. I just studied and found out the cause of it. In her past life she was poorly fed and lived upon begging (I hope Bahu will excuse me for writing this), but her desires were only to the extent of satisfying the hunger. She was a pious lady at the same time attached to God in decimals. This trouble she felt after the death of her husband in the past life. She had one son who used to go with his mother for begging. At that time her son was about nine years of age. After some time she died leaving her son in the care of God. She was in C.P. Her son also lived upon charity and begging after her. This is sufficient and I do not want to go in for further details.

So these troubles of begging and satisfying hunger through difficult means have left impressions upon her. If they are cleaned, she will begin to rise. May Master help me.   (p.116)

I find that when abhyasis come to me at Shahjahanpur there is generally much cleaning necessary, and this imposes a great burden and strain on me, since I have to devote sufficient time to clean the abhyasi before I can start the real spiritual work for which he has come.   (p.135)

Cleaning of the abhyasi is done as a mere formality without applying the force of the preceptor's will. This really means that mere motion of cleaning is gone through, but really it has no effect.   (p.136)

ⁱInstructions to Preceptors

3. Clean the pupil thoroughly. For this it is necessary to 'read' or to 'see' the pupil's spiritual condition. Transmit for a few minutes while concentrating on the condition of the pupil and the condition will be revealed as:

 a) an anatomical map of the person with dark spots or patches which must be removed by applying thought force.

 b) as an idea in your mind that there is grossness at a particular point, or

 c) as a reaction in your own system.

When the reading is clear, clean the pupil by making the thought and applying your will.

4. Clean points A and B thoroughly at every individual sitting. As the cleaning proceeds the points get brighter and brighter.

5. For group sittings, take the pupils in naturally formed groups as they sit, and clean them group by group and then transmit to all of them.

6. For new persons wanting to begin meditation at least two, and sometimes three, sittings will be necessary. In the first sitting clean the heart thoroughly. If it is not completed in the first sitting, take it up again during the second sitting the next day. When cleaning is over, transmit and introduce Master's light into the heart of the pupil. (p.199)

— ❖ —

I am telling you **privately** to clean the grossness of your father, because you are there on the spot to see what is necessary.
(p.208)

Cleaning of the abhyasi is the most important work of the preceptor, but it is done as a mere formality without applying the force of will. This really means that mere motion of cleaning is gone through which does not serve the purpose. At least 10 to 15 minutes should be devoted to cleaning. More attention and time are needed in certain cases.   (p.244)

* Sleeping in the waking state is the common disease in almost all the human beings.

Suppose new souls are coming. After coming into body the thinking developed — both right and wrong. Thus the wrong thoughts and actions debase the souls and hence need cleaning. Since we have degenerated ourselves by our own thinking, cleaning is essential.   (p.279)

It is a pity that we do not read authenticated books, say, raja yoga. Raja yoga sets in when other things accumulated by wrong practices, are gone. Preceptors clean grossness out, but people enwrap it again. So, you have to seek the solution yourself, just as you have to walk on your own legs. Of course, energy is needed for it, for which our help is indispensable, and is ever available.   (p.311)

When you do the cleaning, things are cleaned, to whatever degree it may be. Therefore, you should continue the process. When you, or anybody, do the process of cleaning, a sort of doubt starts in a natural way, because the whole of the things are not cleaned at the same time if they are badly rooted. Really what is cleaned at the time is cleaned, and for the rest you try without doubt.   (p.350)

It is in fact not the rising of thoughts that is annoying to an abhyasi but his own over attention to them which brings him into direct conflict. The reaction thus caused makes thoughts all the more powerful and the trouble is aggravated. It is in fact not the controlling of mind that is suited to our purpose but its right moulding and the proper regulation of its activities. This can be effected not by the use of whip but only by purging out the evil through the process of internal cleaning. This is the only effective way for the transformation of the real being of man.   (p.367)

"In the West many disciples ask, what is the difference between different preceptors. Is an experienced preceptor better than a recent one? Whom to choose? Some disciples say they do not like some preceptors. I think that in the initial stages, the choice of a preceptor does not matter, since the sittings are specifically for cleaning of the heart region. The difficulty comes only later, after one starts the 'yatra' or journey ..."   (p.379)

My Master
Shri P. Rajagopalachari

... You would have experienced that sometimes when you enter a new place you feel disturbances. It may be fear, it may be passion. This is automatic and becomes second nature to a sensitive person. Then by Master's grace, if the power is given, you can 'clean' the place. Just imagine Master's grace is flowing through the place and washing away all the impressions. That is all. You see how easy it is! But faith must be there, and a firm will."   [Babuji](p.18)

... Sometimes I go to a new place where the atmosphere is so bad that I am almost suffocated. Then I have to clean it, otherwise I could not live in it. So we have to do this cleaning wherever we go. That is why I tell my associates that a Master is really a sweeper, doing a sweeper's job. He attracts all the dirt and uncleanliness, and has to clean them off. That is why they say that for a whole country a single saint of calibre is sufficient. He acts like a big cleaner, cleaning the whole country, because all the grossness is attracted to him. You see this 'tamasha' (joke), a Master is really a cleaner! That is why I say that a saint is a target for the world's sorrows. So sometimes we have to control sensitivity so that we are not too much affected. Otherwise a sensitive person will become a victim of his environment.   [Babuji](p.19)

● Later, when we were alone, Master told me that soon after he commenced transmission he got the impression that a monkey was sitting in the group. He opened his eyes and found an abhyasi of long association sitting there. He closed his eyes and in a few moments the same experience was repeated — the monkey was again there! Master once again opened his eyes and found the abhyasi there. Master said, "You know, I could hardly control my laughter. When I opened my eyes this abhyasi was there, when I closed them a monkey was there. Do you know the reason? I will tell you. I examined the case and found that he had been doing Hanuman worship for a very long time, maybe in some past life, and the impressions were there, very strong and deeply buried. During cleaning the impressions must have come to the surface of the mind. Therefore I had the impression of a monkey sitting there!"

Master has given many similar examples of grossness arising out of wrong approaches to worship. In some cases the grossness is deeply embedded, and so hard, that virtually no help can be given. I asked Master how this could happen, that he himself was unable to help. Master replied, "I will tell you. I have had some cases where the heart is surrounded by grossness so hard that it is like a rock. It appears as if the heart is embedded in solid rock. If you give transmission in such cases it will just come back to you." I asked Master whether, in such cases, nothing could at all be done. Was there no way out for them? Master answered, "Well, if the power is used it can be done. There is no doubt about it. But the danger is there that in breaking the grossness the person himself may be affected. The process will have to be very slow, and only complete co-operation on the part of the abhyasi can help him. In such cases I suggest that they pray sincerely to God daily for help. Later on the case can be taken up for deep cleaning." I related to Master a somewhat graphic experience I had had once with an abhyasi. I was carrying out the process of cleaning when, suddenly, a vision came before my eyes, and I saw a giant sewer, bigger than a man, pouring out sewage of such a filthy condition that I was momentarily nauseated. Master said, "Yes, that is the work of the preceptor. I told you a Master is nothing but a sweeper. But the whole problem is only when working in the heart region. Really speaking the heart region is the gutter of humanity. We have to dive into this and do the work. Yes, once the abhyasi progresses and rises to the mind region, then the work becomes a pleasure. After that not much effort is needed. A capable Master can do the work by a mere glance. Now I am telling you one thing. In my own interest I move people quickly out of the heart region. After all who would like to work there longer than necessary? But co-operation of the abhyasi can speed up the process, and save me a great deal of trouble and work."

Master narrated to me another experience relating to cleaning. On that occasion he had gone to Benares, and unwittingly had strayed into a street with an unsavoury reputation. He instinctively felt that he was in the wrong place. At that moment he heard Lalaji's voice asking, "What are you doing in this place?" Master was nonplussed, and answered, "Saheb, I am here by mistake. I do not know where I am." Lalaji said, "Since you are here, let the people of this place derive some benefit from your presence. Clean the atmosphere of this locality as you go." Master laughed and added, "I obeyed Lalaji's orders. Now look at His greatness. He did not chide me for going there. But his love for humanity is seen in his order to me. We must always strive that wherever we may go, we must leave the light of Reality burning there."   (p.89-91)

— ❖ —

● "... Once a person came to me, and what to say of him, I found him already at the fourth point. It was a high level of attainment and showed his work in his past life. He came to me once, but never returned again. His *samskara* must have prevented it. If he had come back his progress was certain. A little cleaning would have made quick progress possible. It is a pity that he never came back. Now who knows how many lives he may need to find the way! ... "   [Babuji](p.104)

— ❖ —

๏ " ... When we take up the heart under our system we ensure that purification goes on side by side with spiritual progress. This cleaning is very important. Really speaking, at the earlier stages of *sadhana* under our *sanstha* it is very important to do this cleaning regularly. As the purification goes on by removing the impression of past *samskaras*, the possibility of progress is opened up. So this cleaning is very important. You remember the example I gave you of a case where I had to clean the impressions of a previous life? You see how deep these *samskaras* lie? It may be necessary to go back even more. That is why I say a true preceptor or trainer is one who can read the past life. Of course this may not be necessary in every case."   [Babuji](p.113)

— ❖ —

๏ " ... It is the *samskaras* which are creating this resistance. Sometimes the *samskaras* are so deep that they are difficult to overcome. Regular cleaning is necessary for a long time. This is the effect of *samskaras* — I mean this resistance. So you see, such persons have to be patient and try to create co-operation. ... "   [Babuji](p.131)

This brings us to the second stage of Master's work — cleaning and purifying the abhyasi to make quick progress possible, and to consolidate that progress. What is it that is cleaned? Master's general answer is that the whole system has to be thoroughly cleaned. This includes the heart and the higher points one after the other. The main work is on the heart and the heart region where much of the *samskaric* residue lies buried in the form of grossness. Master teaches that when we act in any way — the word 'act' being taken in its widest meaning to include all sensory activity and mental activity — the action leaves an 'impression' which is called a *samskara* when it is very deep. It is clear that the superficial impressions are easily cleaned off. It is easy to wipe a slate and clean it. But it is not so with a gramophone record, for instance, where the impressions have been made deep enough to form permanent grooves. When we become 'involved' in our actions the danger of deep impressions being formed is much greater. The accumulated impressions which are in us form the *samskaric* burden of the past. This has to be cleaned by the Master by the use of his own spiritual power. As this cleaning proceeds the abhyasi experiences actual 'lightness' during his meditation sittings.

❧ I had a personal problem in this connection which I once discussed with Master. When I first started meditation a great number of thoughts used to come up and intrude but, on following Master's technique of not attending to thoughts, the inrush of thoughts became progressively reduced until I could experience intervals of thoughtlessness. But, and this was my problem, after a few years of *sadhana* I suddenly found thoughts of a most sordid and vile nature coming during meditation. Naturally I was considerably perturbed because I was apprehensive that this might indicate not progress but regress. Master quickly cleared the problem up for me. He said, "You see, the dust that settles every day on the table can be easily dusted off. It is superficial and easy to remove. Suppose ink has been poured on the table and allowed to soak, then the cleaning is more difficult. So the nature of the impression makes the difference. Now I tell you one more thing. We sometimes have bad thoughts, I mean consciously. We feel ashamed and push them down. Now the very bad or worst thoughts are hidden away deep inside the mind. So in cleaning they may come up last of all. In your case this is what has happened. You should be happy that these vile thoughts have been removed at last. Progress will be quicker now. Do you understand this? It is like a pond. The leaves and dust float on its surface and can be easily removed. But heavy dirt sinks down, and effort is necessary. So in cleaning it comes up last. So there is nothing to worry about. But I am telling you it is important to remove the day's accumulation the same day itself. Otherwise tomorrow it will have become a little more hard and solid, and require more effort. That is why I prescribe daily cleaning by the abhyasis themselves. This process, if correctly followed, will remove the day's accumulation. The rest is the Master's work. So you see the importance of daily cleaning?"

On one occasion, several years after I had commenced *sadhana*, I went to Shahjahanpur. Master had been telling me that my progress was good and that he was generally very satisfied with it. He gave me an individual sitting which lasted over half an hour. At the end of it he said, "Now I have cleaned your system and removed the grossness." I was a bit perturbed to hear this because I felt that there could not be much need for cleaning. I told Master that I had done nothing consciously which could have added grossness to my system. He had also been writing to me praising my progress. I requested him to explain how this grossness had now come into me to need cleaning. Master laughed and said, "You should not worry about this. It was not much, but you know I am a perfectionist and I cannot bear to see even a single dark spot in the system. I will tell you one thing. On a black shirt a dirty patch or spot will not show, but on a clean white shirt even the smallest drop of ink will stand out and invite attention to itself. Anyway it is my concern and you should not worry about it." This ended the discussion.

At a subsequent discussion Master emphasised the importance of cleaning as related to progress. Master said, "By Lalaji's Grace we have a method of training which I can say is of unsurpassed efficacy. Do you know what makes it such a wonderful and easy system? It is the cleaning process followed under Sahaj Marg. Really speaking it is our past impressions which hold us down and create patterns of behaviour which we are unable to modify. We are the slaves of our past. We think we are free to think and act as we like but, truly speaking, this is a fallacy. We are conditioned in everything by the past. Now how to change a person under these conditions? This is Lalaji's greatness that by this process of cleaning he makes it possible to completely remove the effects of the past, in stages of course. You see what a great boon this is. What is the use of telling a person he must change? Of course everyone would like to change, but it is not possible. Why? Because the mind is conditioned by the past. So you see, change can come only by cleaning the mind of past impressions. This makes it possible for the abhyasi to be slowly liberated from his past. Really speaking this is our only bondage. Our past impressions create tendencies in us which we find difficult to change. When the impressions are cleared, the tendency can be changed easily and, in many cases, automatically. Then thought and action become correct and natural. Therefore to transmit is not enough. Cleaning is very important. Otherwise the abhyasi may progress but the danger of fall is always there because the impressions of the past can drag him back. If progress is to be made permanent, purification of the system is essential. That is why I ask our preceptors to pay more attention to this aspect of the work. It is a very important aspect. But much hard work is necessary particularly at the lower stages. So sometimes there is a tendency to ignore this, but then that is a dis-service to the abhyasi. We are here to serve the abhyasi, and if cleaning is neglected then we are not really serving him. This I tell again and again to our preceptors."

    ₒ This subject of cleaning crops up again and again in my discussions with Master. It is a process to which he gives the greatest importance, and to which he also ascribes great efficacy. At one such discussion session I asked Master how long this need for

cleaning would exist. Master laughed and said, "This depends on
you. If there is complete co-operation then the work is easy. Suppose I go on cleaning and the abhyasi goes on adding more and
more grossness, than what can I do?" So you see the abhyasi
must co-operate too. He must modify his life in such a way that it
is helpful to his progress. To remove past accumulations is the
Master's work. But the abhyasi should be alert that he does not
add more grossness by his own thoughts and actions. So this
alertness is necessary. And if the daily process of self-cleaning is
followed, then by Lalaji's grace a stage can be reached when the
formation of impressions no longer takes place, and *samskara*
formation stops.   (p.132-136)

Master said, "As the abhyasi grows, the transmission and
cleaning make yet higher approaches open to him ..."   (p.141)

\ The second group covers all experiences arising from the
cleaning process. Master has stated that when the system of the
abhyasi is cleaned, then the past impressions are removed. When
these impressions surface to the mind then the original experience
or activity which created the impressions is once again created in
the mind. So the abhyasi has an 'experience'. In general the experiences which abhyasis have are of this category. The visions
of gods and goddesses that abhyasis experience during meditation
are of this type. Whenever such an experience comes up, it is an
indication of a past involvement with that particular deity. I have
referred elsewhere to one such experience where Master himself
saw a monkey in the place of an abhyasi. Many abhyasis have
startlingly clear visions of gods or saints. Quite a few make the
tragic mistake of thinking that the goal has been reached, since
their chosen personal god has granted them his *darshan*.   (p.148)

The experiences arising out of cleaning may be numerous, and may last for many years depending on the condition of the abhyasi. The revelatory experiences come when the abhyasi is established on the path, and devotion for the Master has filled his heart. There is no set time for this. It may be the very same day on which one commences abhyas, or never at all.   (p.151)

Sahaj Marg in Europe
Shri P. Rajagopalachari

So the system of Sahaj Marg, which is the name of the yoga system that we practice, accepts any individual human being, whatever may be his present condition or state of mind, because the past, the burden of the past, the Master removes, and the future we create by co-operation with him. The process of removal of the impressions is called cleaning.   (p.72)

In a sense we can think of Sahaj Marg operating in three layers. The lowest is the cleaning of the past impressions by the Master's own power. The middle level is our own effort in meditation and avoiding such thoughts or such activities that can create further impressions. And at the apex we have the most important feature, and that is the system of transmission that is unique to this system.

When the vessel is cleaned we must put something into it. When the human system is similarly purified and cleaned of all the past, it is emptied. Then starts the final process of yoga, which is final not in the sense of time, but final in the sense of culmination. Master starts filling us with his own self.   (p.78-79)

So, in this way, when we train the mind or regulate the mind, naturally and systematically during meditation, no impressions are formed.

Simultaneously the cleaning process is going on. What is the value of that cleaning? Now, it is the past impressions which create in us what Master calls *tendencies...*   (p.83-84)

Master has often said that to begin young is the best thing for spirituality. There are two reasons. The first is, when we are very old we have a much bigger load of past impressions which he has to clean for us, and also what began as tendencies have become habits, have become patterns of life, which we can rarely change.
(p.85)

Babuji: Philosophy is the way of thinking; Yoga is the way of doing; and Realisation is the way of undoing!...

Two ideas came to me, in relation to Master's thought. One: The Sahaj Marg cleaning process is really a process of undoing. Master confirmed this.   (p.100)

On the way Master told H that he had had a very restless night. He said, "I think the cover of my quilt was changed yesterday. I think it must have been used by a licentious person before that. When I went to bed I had a lot of bad thoughts, and this kept me awake and restless for a long time. Finally at about 3 a.m. the idea came to me to clean it, and when I did I slept at once. Now look here! I had not remembered to clean it earlier. This was my foolishness. It is the effect of the environment. So we have to be always alert."   (p.108-109)

The impressions of the past, engraved upon mind and memory, have to be erased. Such impressions are the source of present thoughts and actions. Therefore, sᴜ long as they persist, action along certain lines is compulsive. The cleaning of the system is thus of paramount importance. A bottle which contained oil can be cleaned comparatively easily to become a milk container. But how does one clean a scratched gramophone record? However much we may wipe it, or clean it with detergents, it still continues to play the same jarring tune. Of such scratches and deep cuts is our life composed — scratches of disappointment! Deeper grooves of failure, shame and misery! The deepest grooves of degradation and corruption! Is it then any matter for wonder that the needles of our individual destinies run but in those same worn grooves, repeating everlastingly the same disappointments, the same failures and misery, and the same degradation and corruption? The cleaning here has to go deeper. It involves a remoulding of the system to re-create a new record capable of playing the sublime music that the Maker had originally impressed upon its unblemished surface.

Sahaj Marg lays the greatest emphasis upon the need for such cleaning. All impressions which lie in us, created by our past thoughts and actions, have to be cleaned out thoroughly. The Master does this by using his spiritual power to liberate us from our buried impressions. When this is done we take new birth, as it were. We are spiritually reborn. Superficial physical cleanliness of the human system will not avail us. A deeper cleaning is essential to rid us of the burdens of the past, and these burdens of the past are nothing but the impressions that we have engraved upon ourselves by our wrong thoughts and actions. Such cleaning is therefore liberation from the past in a very real sense...

Once this cleaning is effectively undertaken by a Master of Spiritual calibre, we enter into an unconditioned present...

In the practice of meditation as taught by my Master, this spiritual cleaning is a continuing process. All thoughts and actions create impressions. As they are created they have to be cleaned off. In the beginning of spiritual practice this is more difficult because the past impressions lie deeply buried within us. But as the Master takes charge of the aspirant, he undertakes the cleaning of these deep impressions until we arrive at a stage where few past impressions, if any, exist. Such impressions as do still exist are superficial impressions, easily cleaned off...

Because our work is no longer conditioned by our desires but is undertaken only out of a sense of duty and dedication, impressions cease to be created. The past has already been done away with. The cleaning process of the Sahaj Marg practice has seen to that...

Yoga means Union...

The perfection of the imperfect is what has to be achieved before union is possible. This is achieved by the cleaning process under Sahaj Marg. Now the two have to merge to become one — Yoga is yet to be achieved.   (p.125-130)

In the evening, after one's daily routine of life is completed, Master advises us to sit with eyes closed and to imagine that the Master's Grace is flowing through us removing with it all the day's accumulation of impressions thus wiping off the effect of the day's activities and thoughts. Meticulous practice of this technique ensures that the individual is not adding to the burdens of the past which the Master is quietly cleaning away by his own spiritual power. We are therefore able to progress unimpeded by fresh accumulation of impressions.   (p.132)

❬ Now when you have cleaned something, something has to be put into it. We can clean a bottle but only with the object of replacing the dirt with something clean. What Master now puts into our cleaned purified system is himself, or his spiritual essence, in the form of what we call transmission.   (p.213)

The third factor is what in Sahaj Marg we speak very specifically about — the process of cleaning which refers to the impressions of the past, which are buried in us as *samskaras* as they are called in Sanskrit. In a sense it is these *samskaras* which become the burden tying us down to this existence, being worked upon by gravity, let us say. Now when he cleans us Master refers to what he calls a vacuumization of the inside of our own system, so that something new can be put into it. When you remove something from the system a space is created inside into which he pours his transmission. That is the fourth aspect of the Master's work.

Restricting myself for the time being to this cleaning, I have always wondered why so many sincere, extraordinarily sincere people who practised yogic systems in the past with almost fanatic zeal, subduing every human instinct they had, yet fell short of achieving the goal. Thinking over the past so many years about this, it was only two days ago while I was myself sitting in meditation that the answer came to me. Every one of those aspirants had in some way cleaned himself and created a vacuum. But what is it that is going to fill this vacuum? Please note, when a vacuum is created unless it is attached to a source from which the vacuum chamber can itself be filled up with the appropriate thing, it is only going to attract everything that is outside itself! Now we have vacuum cleaners in our houses and even though it is vacuumized it only picks up the dirt and dust from the carpets on which we expose it. In a chemical plant if you want something to flow from one chamber to another you vacuumize it and connect it to that precise chamber from which you want something to be fed into it. If not, it will only take in the surrounding air and the dust...

This is what happens to a very serious and very practical abhyasi who, without guidance, without connection to the goal, by great effort over very long years of time vacuumizes himself, and finds that everything he is throwing out is coming back into himself. I think this is a matter of simple logic. In those cases where people have had Masters, and have been deeply connected to them by love, by devotion, by emotional attachment of a spiritual nature, all that they could draw from their Master was what the Master had within him...

Therefore it becomes an absolutely important thing that **when we connect ourselves to a Master, the Master must be of that order who can take us to the Ultimate stage of our evolution.** Because, what he does not have in himself he cannot give to us however powerful the vacuum inside us may be...

It thus becomes obvious that by connection with a Master who has in himself the highest ability, the highest achievement, the highest goal that he has achieved for himself by such a connection, the Master can, by the mere and very simple process of emptying my inside, pour himself into me without any effort on my part. This is possible because he cleans my system, he creates a vacuum in me, and by creating this vacuum in me, his Self flows naturally into me. He offers himself. We call this *pranahuti* or offering of the life principle into life. So when we realise that the Master is the cleaner, the Master is the vacuumizer, the Master is the one who comes into me, and thus makes me like himself in every way, we find that He is the goal, we find that He is the way, and we also find that He is the Master who is going to take me through the way to the goal. So in the proper perspective, and with the proper approach to spirituality these three things — the way, the goal, and the guide — they all merge into one entity. And only where such a triumvirate merging into one exists does the possibility of myself too merging into that, and becoming one with that, exist.

I therefore wish to emphasise that it is of the greatest importance that we seek the proper Master, one who has this ultimate connection, who has the ability to clean our insides, to vacuumize our insides. And if this is done there is no question of time, there is no question of effort, there is no question of space. Achievement becomes instantaneous, evolution becomes instantaneous.

We just jump, as it were, from our present mundane existence into the highest realms of spiritual existence.   (p.256-257)

"One major feature of Sahaj Marg is the cleaning of the samskaras. I have been looking for many years for methods and systems which can extend the limits which are normally given to psychotherapy and psychiatry..."

"Why is it a limited method? I think it is because, under the normal conditions, it is impossible to get into the depths of the sub-conscious mind and to really remove the disturbing factor which is disturbing the personality or the life of some one. This is the point I wish to make from my own experiences with the Sahaj Marg system. I can tell you this is the point where Sahaj Marg begins! This is the wonderful thing about Sahaj Marg, that it actually goes much deeper. The cleaning and transmission are techniques and methods able to cross all the borders and all the levels which cannot be crossed under normal conditions. They can therefore clean the whole system and all the depths of the personality in such a way that, after a while, you have real changes of the personality."   (p.276-277)

In its true form, in its ultimate form, love is something which embraces some very fundamental principles. This is founded on old Indian philosophy which says that unless certain things come together love cannot exist. The first is purity. Purity means not merely purity of the body or of the mind, but purity in every aspect of our existence. Purity of thought, purity of action, purity in our interpersonal relationships, purity of the house, not at the cost of the environment but while keeping the environment also pure, all this is necessary. So we have to balance this purity between the inside and the outside. What H said is very very vital here, that the inner cleaning and the outer cleaning should go side by side. That brings us to the first step which is essential — a very vital and all embracing concept that this purity has to pervade every form, every aspect of our life, every function of our life.

(p.281-282)

Blossoms in the East
Shri P. Rajagopalachari

The thought came up automatically in my mind and I seemed to recall, as if in recollection, Master's divine love for his abhyasis, his unfailing courtesy, his quiet generosity, his permanent cheerfulness etc. The thought then came into my mind that this was perhaps an aspect of cleaning too! I felt that even the impressions created in the mind by his qualities had to be erased. Otherwise love for the Master is there, but it is a love conditioned by the existence of these qualities. (p.14)

The result of such an explosion in the human heart is to throw away precisely all the overburden of material life that one had accumulated during his lifetime. But since his spiritual feelings are petrified, and lack refinement, all that the release of the long locked-up finer feelings and nobler sentiments is able to achieve is to build in stone, concrete or steel monuments to his personal failure. At this stage a person's spiritual inclination can find no higher expression. Only this rather negative expression is available. To be able to give proper expression to it, cleaning of all past impressions is essential. Such past impressions are the mental footpaths and highways on which we proceed. Until they are erased, we remain their slaves. This is an important, perhaps the most important, duty of the Master. (p.130)

Now, when our spiritual aspirations open up, we have seen that they can go into gross channels of approach to reality. The cleaning of impressions which I referred to a moment ago, can alone guarantee that newly awakened spiritual impulses go in the right channel or approach.   (p.131)

The second one refers to cleaning of the inner system. The Master and his preceptors are largely active in this, but we have to practise it daily as a measure of co-operation. By this technique all the impressions we have engraved upon ourselves by our past thoughts and actions are erased. Such impressions have to be removed. Otherwise they form the channels for our future thought and activity. Such impressions therefore hold us in bondage. To get freedom, they have got to be removed. When we start our lives we are already following a particular path determined by such impressions of the past. They are strengthened by following the same pattern, over and over again. We do things in a certain way, think in a certain way, not because we want to do so but because we are following a pattern already engraved upon us by past impressions. We have, in a very real sense, very little freedom. It is only when cleaning is effective and impressions are removed that the element of freedom enters our life and we become capable of guiding our lives in a chosen direction. Master is able to do this cleaning for us by the use of his own spiritual powers, and we participate in it, assist in it, by following the technique outlined for us, and by trying to live in such a way that our thoughts and actions don't create further impressions. In this technique both we and the Master are active participants.

     (p.149-150)

The whole process towards Realisation is greatly accelerated by the cleaning process which eradicates the tendencies created by past impressions. We are being purified, while being simultaneously filled with that which should be in us, for us to be spiritual persons.   (p.151)

Then there are various cosmic factors. As Master says great Saints are like vacuum cleaners. They do not draw just the dirt or the uncleanliness or the grossness from individuals. They draw it from the very atmosphere itself. Therefore it is said that if the world has one Saint of calibre it is more than enough, because he sucks into himself all the rubbish that we are throwing out from our lives. So, these are some very important reasons why the Guru — the Master — comes amongst us.   (p.168)

The Garden of Hearts
Shri P. Rajagopalachari

Q: Master! What is the best time for the cleaning process?

PR: Master says that the appropriate time is when the day's work is over.

Q: When an abhyasi is very sincere, is it necessary to do the cleaning?

PR: Suppose you are very sick, can you be cured by just being a sincere patient? It is necessary to take the proper medicines to re-establish health.   (p.109)

H: Just one question about cleaning in the evening. We usually do the prayer — we speak the prayer before cleaning in the evening. Is this correct?

PR: We are told to repeat the prayer only once in the morning; and again only once for the night prayer.

Q: Can it do any harm if we say it before cleaning in the evening?

PR: It is not prescribed by Master and so we should not do it.

(p.137-138)

Q: When we are gathered with the Master and together all day, is it advisable to do one's own practice, for instance meditation if it is morning, or cleaning if it is in the evening?

PR: You always meditate in the morning according to the system prescribed by the Master. If you are having the evening sitting here, then there is no need to separately do the cleaning. The night prayer meditation should also be done by you before you go to bed.

(p.138)

I have found, during our travels from 1972 to 1980, that there is a perceptible change in the attitude of the Westerners to prayer. There is more acceptance. This is because of prayer and cleaning, both by ourselves and from our preceptors; and because of this, this problem is decreasing.

(p.148)

Everything that happens to us is as a result of our samskaras. Master is giving us progress. In the act of giving us our spiritual progress, there is this need to do the cleaning and removal of samskaras, along with the *bhoga* to the extent that an abhyasi can bear.

(p.161)

As far as the duties of a preceptor are concerned, a preceptor is supposed to basically concern himself with the cleaning of the abhyasi. Master is emphasising this aspect more and more because unless the cleaning is done in as systematic and efficient a way as is possible, it becomes difficult, if not impossible, for Master to give spiritual advancement to the particular abhyasi. Perhaps some preceptors are not aware that when transmission is given, if the cleaning has not been done to prepare the abhyasi to receive it, it will only strengthen the tendencies already latent in him or her. So this cleaning is the most important part of a preceptor's work. Master says that we should devote at least eighty percent of our time to the cleaning of the abhyasi. After the cleaning is over, the preceptor transmits. When we receive new persons to be admitted as abhyasis, it becomes necessary to give them at least three sittings, one on each day. The first two sittings are generally devoted entirely to cleaning. There is no transmission. It is on the third day that the transmission is started, after the concerned preceptor is satisfied that sufficient cleaning has been done so that transmission can be begun.   (p.173-174)

Preceptors are abhyasis. For himself each preceptor is only an abhyasi on the path. He is a preceptor only to the other abhyasis. So preceptors also need cleaning; preceptors also need transmission; and the first sign of self-importance and ego is when one preceptor does not go to another preceptor for sittings. It does not matter who the preceptor is. All preceptors need sittings, cleaning and transmission.   (p.179-180)

Under Master's instructions the difference between cleaning, and the meditation upon grossness which is what many abhyasis are found to be doing, was carefully and clearly brought out. The importance of daily cleaning was also emphasised, pointing out that if this is not done every day, we will add the impressions of each day's thoughts and activities and so add to the burden of our grossness, and thus increase Master's burden of work.   (p.244)

Babuji in Shahjahanpur — 1971-1975
Transcriptions

Q: Unless one has a vacuum grace cannot descend into him?

Babuji: And that is by grossness, and I am telling you, I devote so much time in removing it, and I am having very good results also. So most of the time I devote in cleaning you. And of course transmission is alongside. So transmission is moulded for some specific purpose, that that it works. Suppose in this very transmission you mould it that I may become rich. It will not work there also. It is a sort of power. Moulding is your work.   (p.23)

Q: I am like many other Americans, I'm very tense and nervous, and very tight in the stomach area and the breathing has been very shallow. Is there anything that I and other people with a similar problem could do to correct it?

Babuji: No, if there is disease, the doctor is there. And this is not any spiritual disease, I'm telling you. And has no concern with it. Spirituality, spirituality... even cures the disease, not produces. This cleaning system, I am telling you, so many diseases are gone.

So I am telling you, there are two cases. I was also cleaning them. In one night the pleurisy disappeared ..., and some people have related that such and such a disease has been diminished, or has gone. Automatically it will result. And suppose if anybody has got disease. And along with that process of cleaning, you think that disease is also going out. It will have very good effect ... you can use it for health also. But again the press is there for realisation. That is this method has the only, this purpose, that you may realise God. Alongside so many things are corrected.

(p.33)

Babuji: So the mind was there, now you began to think otherwise also, and that was the cause of sufferings. God is not responsible. But he is very kind. He does not want that that thing remain in you. So it is burst into the diseases or some difficulties. Only to clean it, I myself observed, after some ailments, fever and so on. I found myself better.   (p.54)

Q: Well, can the misery collected in earlier lives be reduced by changing over our actions?

Babuji: No, I am telling you, the method of cleaning, and Master also cleans, that reduces. Of course something comes for *bhogam*, but so many things are gone.

Q: Does *bhogam* ... the effect will be lessened?

Babuji: Lessened.

So here in Sahaj Marg system formation of further samskaras, what you call impressions, are stopped automatically. That you should not keep anything for future. Do not build anything for future. So one thing is stopped, now the other thing, so by cleaning system or by fever or by any other disease, you may have it.
                                    (p.56)

Q: Thomas said that in Denmark long back, once, we talked about visions and so on. If visions were real visions or self created or something, then Thomas said, I think every single vision is only cleaning!

Babuji: That is correct.

Q: Correct?! But there will be also some higher visions isn't it, some message or something?

Babuji: Maybe, I am telling you, mostly they are past ... There are two types of visions: imaginative and divine. So really, generally I may say, they are having imaginative and not divine. Divine, then it is... you will feel something, all around you. That is divine, divine thoughts. (p.81-82)

Babuji: You clear all the points. And Thomas will write and you all sit together and correct it.

Q: Then I think some fear will be in some people, when they sit for meditation and have cleaning also. They will think, what am I being shaped into?

Babuji: There, tell him the method. What is prescribed, should be done. And that will bring the result you want.

Q: And they can check up by feeling, the peace and good things come?

Babuji: No, no. What is coming, let it come. Don't disturb it, what is coming. Whether it will be good or bad. If it is good, it is leaving its own centre, and coming out.

A bottle; cork is there, you put wine in it, it will go,... if you take out the cork and you will pour out the wine. And when you want to take it out you will, what you call ... take out the cork and you do in this way. That is, the way it enters, that is the way to come out. Wine entered into the bottle, in this way, when you take ...

Q: That is the cleaning process you explain?

Babuji: No, I am telling you this. And when you want, that, to empty the bottle, you will do the reverse process. Similarly here — at that time, anything which is coming into you, that is coming, coming out from the bottle, it was imprisoned. Coming out from the bottle, and these impressions are very near the heart, so they come down. There will ... there must all will be cleaned. Otherwise no freedom. (p.95-96)

Q: Thomas was asking in Denmark, to ask you, how we should tell abhyasis to clean themselves, when they do cleaning.

Babuji: The way is given there. The way is given there. Just tell him to take out the grossness and throw it behind it. It is a sort of automatic suggestion also. Oh no, I mean suggestion also, and at the same time work also.

You think — not only think — but take out all this grossness, think it is going out. And actually feeling that it is going out. That is going ...   (p.115)

— ❖ —

Q: Do you have pains?

Babuji: Well, this is on accord of the past actions. We sometimes tease others, sometimes we use vulgar language, sometimes we beat, all the effects is there. And God wants that you may be clear of all these things. So he sends the disease or it bursts out into disease, the same impressions which you have, in order to clean them. Unless its result is over, means you cannot do anything.

Really, Nature is very kind to us. If there are such things, which I have just explained, impressions of the past actions, now in order to clean that, they are burst out into disease.

Q: Yes.

Babuji: So that, that unwanting thing may not remain in your body. But if transmigration is correct we have been here for millions of years and billions of years. We have made so many samskaras, so many impressions and many of them came under, what you call, '*bhogam*'. Brought their result and we have formed again ... so this cycle is going on.

What happens in Sahaj Marg system after if ... if faith is correct, and abhyas is going on well, you will stop formation of samskaras further. Your past is there, even by cleaning system, or by some other system. Some will may be cleaned and some will remain … but future is over. (Hindi: So that means), a part of the battle you have won. (p.139-140)

Babuji: An engineer, he told me after 2, 3 years because, "I am very much healthy since I adopted this method." It is useful for health also. Many diseases go away, I am telling you, I was cleaning one man, I did not know that he was suffering from pleurisy. But, it appears something like that, I said it may be grossness, let it remove. And I removed it and in the morning, he came, "I'm all right." In one night he was cured. And there are two such cases. This cleaning system, this of course takes out diseases also. (p.164)

Babuji: Oh yes, heart is the nucleus of the human body. And it functions, it pumps out blood also. So when we are in meditation, or in the thought of God, now that effects the heart also. So cleaning is needed for your purpose, better for the heart. And blood moves into the body … with that idea. So it brings piety.
(p.170)

Q: Master is it so that not only our bad things have to be cleaned away but also our good things?

Babuji: No, along cleaning, grossness, you remove the grossness. Or if you have got some vicious thought, bad thoughts, well alongside cleaning is also. They are also consumed.

Q: But when a man becomes zero, doesn't it mean that also all his good things have left?

Babuji: Yes, yes nothingness, I have written, translation, nothingness. That this … You feel that there is nothing there. A sort of a state which … I do not find the words … I will have to coin quote, Silence without silence. (p.173)

Proceedings of the Seminar on Sahaj Marg
Vorauf - Munich, Germany, April 27th to May 4th, 1985
Shri P. Rajagopalachari

Now we take up the second thing, which is the evening cleaning process. It is to be done when our whole day's work is over, not before that. During the day's activities and thoughts, we accumulate so many impressions. By doing the cleaning when the day's work is over, we try as far as possible to get rid of that day's impressions. So essentially, the evening cleaning process is to remove the accumulation of impressions gathered during that day. The older and deeper accumulation which is more gross they are not just impressions, they have become grossness — that has to be dealt with by the Master and the preceptors. The way of doing your cleaning is to sit comfortably like in the morning meditation, and to imagine that the day's impressions are going out from behind in the form of smoke or vapour. Now the word imagine should not be misunderstood, because it is a very active process in which we use our will power to remove our own impressions. In the morning meditation there is no use of the will power, please note carefully. The cleaning process involves, very specifically, our will power.   (p.37)

Having got a certain degree of ability to regulate the mind, we have to take the aid of the cleaning process. Because of our tendencies and our habits, all these are precisely the result of samskaras in us. Unless they are cleaned off, there is no point in having a regulated mind at our disposal. The process has to be done very systematically, and with the application of our will power. It removes the basis which is formed in us in the past, and which manifests as present tendencies. Progressive regulation of the mind helps us in not forming further samskaras by gaining a certain degree of control over that mind ourselves. Meditation, and the cleaning process, balance each other, support each other for our evolution. Meditation in itself, without cleaning, is to my mind useless. It would be like having a powerful car bogged down in slime and mud. And cleaning, by itself, is like having a beautiful road with a car on it without any engine. There is a progressive refinement of the motive power in man, which is his mind, which produces his thoughts. And the cleaning removes all the impediments in the way of that progress. This is to be remembered very carefully because we will find that in the religious history of humanity, meditation has been going on from time immemorial. There is not any very great record of achievement. Because, as Babuji explained, whatever be your progress in meditation, if the samskaras are not removed, they remain as seeds which can come out and flower when the appropriate environment is created for it. That is how even those who rose to very high levels have often fallen, because at that level the samskaras suddenly found an environment proper for their flowering, and they blossomed out.

The other point is that so long as the samskaras are there, if you have more power, the tendencies become more powerful. So, as Babuji explained, if you transmit to a thief, he will become a perfect thief." So that is the very great importance of the cleaning system in our system.

Now that is the practical aspect. What are we to do in all this? The first responsibility is to do the practice thoroughly and systematically, regularly. Morning meditation, evening cleaning, night prayer-meditation, they must be done every day irrespective of whether you have sittings with preceptors or not. The second thing is to try and develop Constant Remembrance, which will come in any case if the practice is systematic. Master has clarified when constant remembrance becomes established, then meditation loses its importance. As an example, I can say it is like focusing a microscope on an object. Because cleaning removes the objects which we don't need, meditation regulates the mind and the two are put together, as one. (p.41-43)

The Principles of Sahaj Marg, Volume I
Shri P. Rajagopalachari

So the system of Sahaj Marg, which is the name of the yoga system that we practise, accepts any individual human being, whatever may be his present condition or state of mind, because the past, the burden of the past, the Master removes, and the future we create by co-operation with him. The process of removal of the impressions is called 'cleaning'.

You will all appreciate that there is no use in removing the impressions of the past if we are going to continue creating further impressions by thoughts and actions. So our participation in this yogic teaching is to mould our lives in such a way that we do not create more impressions, and thus we avoid creating a further past for the future, because everything becomes the past. Today is the past for tomorrow.   (p.72-73)

That now brings me to the most important and fundamental point in Sahaj Marg. In a sense we can think of Sahaj Marg as operating in three layers. The lowest is the cleaning of the past impressions by the Master's own power. The middle level is our own effort in meditation and avoiding such thoughts or such activities that can create further impressions. And at the apex we have the most important feature, and that is the system of transmission that is unique to this system.

When the vessel is cleaned, we must put something into it. When the human system is similarly purified and cleaned of all the past, it is emptied. Then starts the final process of yoga, which is final not in the sense of time, but final in the sense of culmination. Master starts filling us with his own self. This process is called *pranahuti* in Sanskrit, which means 'life offering' or 'offering of life'.   (p.77-78)

To humanise the animal-human being is then the first step in spiritual practice. As my Master states it, animal-man has to become human-man or man-man first, before he can think of further development to the perfect-man. To do this the individual's tendencies have got to be corrected and oriented in the proper direction. The impressions of the past, engraved upon mind and memory, have to be erased. Such impressions are the source of present thoughts and actions. Therefore, so long as they persist, action along certain lines is compulsive. The cleaning of the system is thus of paramount importance. A bottle which contained oil can be cleaned comparatively easily to become a milk-container. But how does one clean a scratched gramophone record? However much we may wipe it, or clean it with detergents, it still continues to play the same jarring tune. Of such scratches and deep cuts is our life composed — scratches of disappointment! Deeper grooves of failure, shame and misery! The deepest grooves of degradation and corruption! Is it then any matter for wonder that the needles of our individual destinies run but in those same worn grooves, repeating everlastingly the same disappointments, the same failures and misery, and the same degradation and corruption? The cleaning here has to go deeper. It involves a remoulding of the system to re-create a new record capable of playing the sublime music that the Maker had originally impressed upon its unblemished surface.

Sahaj Marg lays the greatest emphasis upon the need for such cleaning. All impressions which lie in us, created by our past thoughts and actions, have to be cleaned out thoroughly. The Master does this by using his spiritual power to liberate us from our buried impressions. When this is done, we take new birth, as it were. We are spiritually reborn. Superficial physical cleanliness of the human system will not avail us. A deeper cleaning is essential to rid us of the burdens of the past, and these burdens of the past are nothing but the impressions that we have engraved upon ourselves by our own wrong thoughts and actions. Such cleaning is therefore liberation from the past in a very real sense. We enter into a present unconditioned by a past. Hitherto our present represented nothing but the inexorable culmination of tendencies and trends established in the past. And the future could be nothing but the further inexorable trend of the same tendencies continued beyond the present. We see therefore the effect of the past on the future! Once this cleaning is effectively undertaken by a Master of Spiritual calibre, we enter into an unconditioned present — a present, therefore, which can be correctly used to control and achieve a pre-determined future goal. And that goal is the goal of perfection.

In the practice of meditation as taught by my Master, this spiritual cleaning is a continuing process. All thoughts and actions create impressions. As they are created, they have to be cleaned off. In the beginning of spiritual practice this is more difficult because the past impressions lie deeply buried within us. But as the Master takes charge of the aspirant, he undertakes the cleaning of these deep impressions until we arrive at a stage where few past impressions, if any, exist. Such impressions as do still exist are superficial impressions, easily cleaned off. (p.85-88)

Because our work is no longer conditioned by our desires but is undertaken only out of a sense of duty and dedication, impressions cease to be created. The past has already been done away with. The cleaning process of the Sahaj Marg practice has seen to that. It is as if the past never was. We have entered a present where our thoughts and actions are no longer creating a past which will condition the unborn future. The present is eternal without a past to weigh it down. We have entered a life-dimension which the ancient seers of India, the *rishis*, called the 'eternal present'. Now begins the final approach to the realisation of our goal.

Yoga means Union. Two things cannot unite when they are not fitted for each other. If one is imperfect to start with, it has to be corrected and remoulded and made perfect before it can have union with the perfect one. Therefore yoga, as union, is the culmination of spiritual practice, and not merely a practice itself, as commonly represented. The perfection of the imperfect is what has to be achieved before union is possible. This is achieved by the cleaning process under Sahaj Marg. Now the two have to merge to become one — yoga is yet to be achieved.   (p.88-89)

What the aspirant is taught to do is to sit in meditation in the morning at a suitable time, seated in a convenient posture. The process is to be repeated once again at bed-time and, in between, Master prescribes a cleaning process in which the aspirant has to clean out the daily accumulation of impressions which in Sanskrit we call *samskara*.   (p.90)

In the evening, after one's daily routine of life is completed, Master advises us to sit with eyes closed and to imagine that the Master's Grace is flowing through us removing with it all the day's accumulation of impressions thus wiping off the effect of the day's activities and thoughts. Meticulous practice of this technique ensures that the individual is not adding to the burdens of the past which the Master is quietly cleaning away by his own spiritual power. We are therefore able to progress unimpeded by fresh accumulation of impressions.   (p.91)

Ours is a simple system. It has just three elements in its practice. These are prayer, meditation and cleaning. When a system is so simple as to have just two or three elements in it, then all the elements are essential to the system. If even one element is lacking or is discarded, the system will probably be ineffective in its functioning. In Sahaj Marg practice, we cannot afford to discard any of these elements if the efficacy of the system is not to be impaired.   (p.93)

Now evolution has two forces. This is generally not appreciated by most people. There is a push from the back and there is a pull from the front. Because if there is an evolutionary goal already laid down in the very far past when creation was brought into existence, then the very first organism which was created had only the pull of evolution, and there was nothing to push it from behind. But as life forms advanced on the evolutionary path, they managed to create a large past for themselves, a historical past which is not so bad, but also a past of impressions which Don has already told you we call *samskaras*. Now it is precisely this past which, instead of pushing us from behind, manages to pull us back from behind. So the *samskara* is a very important thing because it acts in an anti-evolutionary way. Instead of having a push from the back and a pull from the front, we have a pull from the front and an op-posing pull from the back so that we are held powerlessly in a situation which we cannot overcome. This pull from the back is precisely what we have to overcome, because the pull from the front is always acting on us. If the pull from the back is removed by a Master who can remove our impressions, then the attractive or the full power of the evolutionary goal already established acts on us without resistance from us. Therefore the cleaning of the impressions of the past is of the highest importance in any system of Yoga.   (p.99-100)

My Master has often remarked that in the East, where people are so dirty outside, they seem to have an inner spiritual cleanliness which seems to be lacking in people of the advanced nations who are very clean outside but have a lot of grossness inside. I have deliberately used the word grossness because grossness in not uncleanliness *per se*. Now it is this inner gross-ness that is a bar to our advancement on the spiritual path. Hitherto, this subject of inner cleanliness has been largely neglected. Even advanced yogic systems, such as the Hatha Yoga and other systems, have restricted their efforts more to the perfection of the physical system than to the perfection of the inner life of man. I think it is one of the unique features of my Master's system of Sahaj Marg that the greatest importance is given to the cleaning of the inner system, the spiritual system, of man. This grossness, my Master teaches, is an accumulation of the impressions of the past.

...Now when we come to practice the Sahaj Marg system of yoga the first thing that the Master impresses upon us, which is at the same time the most important, is that these past impressions must be removed from our mind. (p.108-109)

Now, when you have cleaned something, something has to be put into it. We can clean a bottle but only with the object of re-placing the dirt with something clean. What Master now puts into our cleaned purified system is himself, or his spiritual essence, in the form of what we call transmission. (p.112-113)

The third factor is what in Sahaj Marg we speak very specifi-cally about — the process of cleaning which refers to the im-pressions of the past, which are buried in us as *samskaras* as they are called in Sanskrit. In a sense it is these *samskaras* which be-come the burden tying us down to this existence, being worked upon by gravity, let us say. Now when he cleans us Master refers to what he calls a vacuumization of the inside of our own system, so that something new can be put into it. When you remove something from the system a space is created inside into which he pours his transmission. That is the fourth aspect of the Master's work.

Restricting myself for the time being to this cleaning, I have always wondered why so many sincere, extraordinarily sincere, people who practised yogic systems in the past with almost fa-natic zeal, subduing every human instinct they had, yet fell short of achieving the goal. Thinking over the past so many years about this, it was only two days ago, while I was myself sitting in meditation that the answer came to me. Everyone of those aspirants had in some way cleaned himself and created vacuum. But what is it that is going to fill this vacuum? Please note, when a vacuum is created unless it is attached to a source from which the vacuum chamber can itself be filled up with the appropriate thing, it is only going to attract everything that is outside itself!

(p.135-136)

When we connect ourselves to the wrong source, the very process of vacuumizing ourselves can lead to our degradation — I don't mean in moral values, I mean in the sense of evolutionary degradation — rather than to the uplift that we are so earnestly trying for. It thus becomes obvious that by connection with a Master who has in himself the highest ability, the highest achievement, the highest goal that he has achieved for himself by such a connection, the Master can, by the mere and very simple process of emptying my inside, pour himself into me without any effort on my part. This is possible because he cleans my system, he creates a vacuum in me, and by creating this vacuum in me, his Self flows naturally into me. He offers himself. We call this *pranahuti* or offering of the life principle into life. So when we realise that the Master is the cleaner, the Master is the vacuumizer, the Master is the one who comes into me and thus makes me like himself in every way, we find that He is the goal, we find that He is the way, and we also find that He is the Master who is going to take me through the way to the goal. ...

I therefore wish to emphasize that it is of the greatest importance that we seek the proper Master, one who has this ultimate connection, who has the ability to clean our insides, to vacuumize our insides. And if this is done there is no question of time, there is no question of effort, there is no question of space. Achievement becomes instantaneous, evolution becomes instanta-neous.

We just jump, as it were, from our present mundane existence into the highest realms of spiritual existence.   (p.138-139)

In its true form, in its ultimate form, love is something which embraces some very fundamental principles. This is founded on old Indian philosophy which says that unless certain things come together love cannot exist. The first is purity. Purity means not merely purity of the body or of the mind, but purity in every aspect of our being, in every aspect of our existence. Purity of thought, purity of action, purity in our interpersonal relationships, purity of the house not at the cost of the environment but while keeping the environment also pure, all this is necessary. So we have to balance this purity between the inside and the outside. What H said is very vital here, that the inner cleaning and the outer cleaning should go side by side. That brings us to the first step which is essential — a very vital and all embracing concept that this purity has to pervade every form, every aspect of our life, every function of our life.   (p.142-143)

We all know that most millionaires tend to give away their millions in later life. They establish charitable foundations, build hospitals, erect homes for the poor, build temples, churches or mosques and so on. I used to wonder why people who have worked so feverishly all their lives to accumulate wealth should, as feverishly, try to throw it all away later on, in their lives. I think part of the answer is in the feelings of guilt — but it is only a part of the answer. I think the repressed finer feelings and nobler aspirations — the hallmarks of a truly human being — hidden deep in the heart, one day build up so much pressure that, in a moment of weakness they explode. The result of any explosion is the same. All overburden is blasted off! The result of such an explosion in the human heart is to throw away precisely all the overburden of material life that one had accumulated during his lifetime. But since his spiritual feelings are petrified, and lack refinement, all that the release of the long locked-up finer feelings and nobler sentiments is able to achieve is to build in stone, concrete or steel monuments to his personal failure. At this stage a person's spiritual inclination can find no higher expression. Only this rather negative expression is available. To be able to give proper expression to it, cleaning of all past impressions is essential. Such past impressions are the mental footpaths and highways on which we proceed. Until they are erased, we remain their slaves. This is an important, perhaps the most important, duty of the Master.   (p.165-166)

Now, when our spiritual aspirations open up, we have seen that they can go into gross channels of approach to Reality. The cleaning of impressions which I referred to, a moment ago, can alone guarantee that newly awakened spiritual impulses, go in the right channel or approach. So here we meet with the second imperative, the imperative need of a Master. Who can be a Master? My Master says, "Look for one who can guide you to the highest. Don't be satisfied with anything less than that." Such a guide alone knows the way, having travelled the whole way himself. You may call him Master, Yogi, Saint, or anything else, but he remains a guide, whatever else he may be to us, and for himself. After cleaning our system of past impressions and thus, in a very real sense, lightening us, he takes us on the road which leads us to our goal.   (p.167)

This is the first technique of Sahaj Marg.

The second one refers to cleaning of the inner system. The Master and his preceptors are largely active in this but we have to practise it daily, as a measure of co-operation. By this technique, all the impressions we have engraved upon ourselves by our past thoughts and actions are erased. Such impressions have to be removed. Otherwise they form the channels for our future thought and activity. Such impressions therefore hold us in bondage. To get freedom, they have got to be removed. When we start our lives we are already following a particular path determined by such impressions of the past. They are strengthened by following the same pattern, over and over again. We do things in a certain way, think in a certain way, not because we want to do so but because we are following a pattern already engraved upon us by past impressions. We have, in a very real sense, very little freedom. It is only when cleaning is effective and impressions are removed that the element of freedom enters our life and we become capable of guiding our lives in a chosen direction. Master is able to do this cleaning for us, by the use of his own spiritual powers, and we participate in it, assist in it, by following the technique outlined for us, and by trying to live in such a way that our thoughts and actions don't create further impressions. In this technique, both we and the Master are active participants.

(p.178-179)

The whole process towards Realisation is greatly accelerated by the cleaning process which eradicates the tendencies created by past impressions. We are being purified, while being simultaneously filled with that which should be in us, for us to be spiritual persons. (p.180)

It seems that our power to stop progress is much greater than our power to promote progress. I have always been concerned that the power to spread evil, the power to spread disease, the power to spread ignorance, this power seems to be so much more powerful than the power to do good. I asked Master about this once. Master smiled and said, "There is no such power, I mean evil power or power to do bad things. Our power acts in such ways because of the tendencies which guide the use of these powers. The tendencies are nothing but the working of our *samskaras*. It is therefore our own creation." This emphasises the necessity for our own cleaning, both by ourselves in our daily routine as well as in cleaning sessions with preceptors.   (p.186)

The Principles of Sahaj Marg, Volume II
Shri P. Rajagopalachari

The moral of this is that the Divine, or Divinity, manifests and reveals itself only as its wish, and can be 'known' only when a revelation takes place. The revelation comes not as a result of yogic or other practices, but as a result of the Master's will to reveal Himself — and it is a very very important fact that **love** alone can compel (yes, **compel**) the Master to do this.

But does this mean that spiritual practices are useless? No. It is the practice or sadhana that prepares the human mind to accept understanding when it comes. It does this by the process of 'cleaning' by which all past impressions are wiped off, transforming the mind into a pure instrument to accept what comes to it in meditation. A normal human mind rarely views any fact or phenomenon as an isolated bit of information input. All judgments (even legal ones) are on the basis of past precedents — what we normally accept as 'experience'. It takes a lot of understanding to realise that this so-called 'experience' most often acts against us by preconditioning us to think and feel in intellectual and emotional ruts, and robs us of the facility of 'pure' action, where each act is a pure act of creation, guided by the parameters of the moment alone, and totally untrammelled by the past. This is what spiritual practice helps us to achieve, thereby endowing us with the ability and willingness to accept revelation when it comes.

(p.47)

The Principles of Sahaj Marg, Volume III
Shri P. Rajagopalachari

So let us make very sure, brothers and sisters — all of you, the learned, the literate, the highly educated — it is time, you see that education is only a veneer. The basic intelligence of all is guaranteed. God does not play tricks with human beings. He has given us *pancha indriyas.* The sensitivity may be lacking. That is because we have put on coloured glasses. Remove them, which is being done for you every day by our devoted preceptors, who are giving you the cleaning again and again, which we destroy — the effects of which we destroy by taking the glasses again and putting them on.

All this talk of Prarabdha, Sanchita, it is all you know, so much trivial, trash to be consigned to the waste paper basket. I have the Divine at my service, and I make bold to say that He is there, and He says "With a glance Lalaji could have transformed and could have liberated, it required but a glance from His eyes." These are the words which Babuji used. I have known Babuji doing it Himself too. So when you come to this aspect and we still keep harping on samskaras, and tendencies, and intelligence and lack of it, I am only sorry to say that we are now not only carrying the burdens of our education, the burdens of our wealth, the burdens of our culture, but we have, in some intangible way become proud of them.

So let us shake off the pride first, so that we may get rid of the burdens, because only then shall we see them as bondages to our understanding, as limitations to our understanding; because we see a biologist talks of God in the biological way, a scientist talks in the way of science, an artist takes pictures of Him. What is it that is the reality behind all these? (p.87-88)

I stress the word 'participation' because I deny that a human being has any possibility of growth by himself. Given the sam-

skaras, given the awful burden of samskaras that we have brought
with us, it is like expecting a stone to do something by itself. We
are as immovable, as incapable of self motion or movement, as a
stone is today because our inner samskara is so awful in its gross
tendencies, that any individual who thinks that he is free to do as
he chooses, is blind. If he thinks he is moving, if he thinks he is
speaking, if he thinks he is acting, yes; he is acting like a loco-
motive under the power of steam — our steam being the com-
pulsion of the samskaras that are in us, which makes one become
a scholar, he doesn't know why he becomes a scholar; another
becomes an artist, he doesn't know why he becomes an artist;
another becomes a doctor, he also doesn't know why. A man who
becomes something and doesn't know why he became that, is
under a compulsive existence. He is under the pressure of compulsive forces locked up in him — no better than a steam loco-
motive which goes on and on until the steam pressure is
exhausted, and it can move us no more. But when the Almighty is
given a seat in the heart, and the cleaning takes place and the
samskaric burden is removed, the first traces of freedom begin;
we can now take a positive hand in guiding our own evolution,
we get into the mainstream of evolutionary existence, which
God's will dominates, which His purpose guides, and the Desti-
nation which is Himself, is there.   (p.142-143)

So we are in that tradition where we have not been trained to
accept Reality as such. We have been conditioned to accept
things either tastefully decorated, or couched in acceptable language, or dressed suitably and, in that way, from hoary ages of
the past, Reality has been covered up; Reality has been occluded,
as it were, and today we have to search for it in the mass of confusion, in the mass of beauty, in the confusion of language, so
that our mind is no longer able to grasp Reality in its naked
condition. Therefore the need for speeches and, much more important, the need for cleaning.

Now, we have all been hearing so much about the spiritual cleaning that the Master is doing, the preceptors are doing, and that we ourselves are expected to do every day, in the evening. That is the internal cleaning of the samskaras which have already been formed. But we do not realise that we have to co-operate in a different way, in a continuous cleaning process, where we should try to rid ourselves of all these social and cultural conditionings of the past — that a thing must look beautiful to be really good, that food must taste well to be really good, that the language of the speaker must be brilliant for his thoughts to be good. All these small conditionings, we have to reject. (p.161-162)

The Principles of Sahaj Marg, Volume IV
Shri P. Rajagopalachari

So, the way from what we are, to what we ought to be, is the process of evolution. And, that growth, that evolution, is supported by transmission in our system. Because with that He pours Himself into us, *after* He has cleaned us sufficiently, as otherwise the transmission only serves to make our own latent tendencies more and more powerful, and perhaps propel us in the same direction, faster and faster, to speedier destruction. (p.135)

But we wonder, you see, "how a sage like Viswamitra, practising for twenty thousand years, and we doing the same thing for one hour, how can we achieve it?" We place a limitation on the practice which is given to us! Who creates the problems? *We* create it ourselves. It is our foolishness, that when the Master says, " Meditate one hour in the morning; clean yourselves for thirty minutes; and have the prayer meditation for ten minutes," we begin to doubt it and say, "How is it possible?" On the contrary we should be happy and say, "Well, here is a system which poor Viswamitra did not have! If he had it, he need not have struggled for twenty thousand years."   (p.147)

You see, periodically, like we have an oil bath once a week and take off the dry skin, there seems to be the need for a cosmic cleaning once in a way, and it comes. So we must accept it when it comes.   (p.170)

The Principles of Sahaj Marg, Volume V
Shri P. Rajagopalachari

So, please remember, we are here not for our personal aggrandisement. Our growth is for His sake, our ennoblement is for His sake, our spiritual elevation is for His sake; and if at all we are ever going to be divinised, that too is for His sake.

So those who will remember this and who take it to their heart, will, I am sure, by His grace, develop very fast. But those who do it out of personal ego, "I want to be a rishi or I want to be a saint" — well, Master will help them too! But the first help He has to do to them is to remove their ignorance and their arrogance from their minds. And, I pray that Master may serve us most by doing this first, that is, so to say, the service we need most. Because people often question: "How is it that such and such a person is like this; and, this man who is said to be so high, is also like this?" It is precisely because notwithstanding His transmission, notwith-standing the cleaning that is going on, we are holding on to our own foolish human ideas that, "I am what I am and I have a right to choose and I have a right to dictate," and God says, "Fine! Exercise it! Make sure, not too long! Because the more you do it, the longer you will be away from me." So like a son returning home in the dark, we should run, you see! (p.26)

You see that when you clean a man, how do you bring about transformation in a man? You know the beautiful story of a great Caliph. He set up an art competition. He said such and such will be the prize for the best entry. There were hundreds of entries. Then came a Chinese team, and everybody was awed, because of the greatest painters. And the last was an Iranian team. And they got two walls of a room with a partition in between; a curtain. So the Chinese team was asking for fabulous paints, golden dust, silver dust. Thirty days was the time given. And they were working twenty-four hours, round the clock, and asking for more and more material, glittering things, polish, emerald, rubies, what not. The other people (Iranian Sufi team) were asking for many mundane things — the Caliph could not even imagine how they could be applied to art: "Anyway, let them do it, we will judge on the thirty first day." On the thirty-first day, after judging everything, he came to the Chinese painting. He was gasping with wonder at how this could be produced! It was a stupendous marvel. And for about half an hour, he was just gazing, he had to be reminded: "Lord, there is one more painting, the last one to be judged." Reluctantly he said, "Yes. Let me see it." They pulled the curtain. And he swooned in wonder! All that the other group of men had done was to polish the surface so beautifully that it was a reflection of the Chinese painting! And it was better than the original thing.

You don't have to create! So, Master's first step is cleaning in Sahaj Marg. If you want to get milk, don't you wash the vessel first? So transformation is first by removal of things and then by elevation of the thing itself. (p.120-121)

So there is no use in Sahaj Marg being practised and after this 45 minutes or one hour meditation we go around merrily doing everything that we were doing and then trying to clean away everything in the evening cleaning. It is a very happy method! So that is not what Lalaji or Babuji intended for us. They intended that Sahaj Marg should be a crystal introduced into our system, to make us crystallise into some sort of a spiritual personality which will practise what it preaches, first by itself, then for others.

(p.156)

The Principles of Sahaj Marg, Volume VI
Shri P. Rajagopalachari

...we tend to live multiple lives, we are something to our families, something to our workers, something to our friends, something to our lovers, something to ourselves and something which we cannot even face within ourselves. And that is the ultimate tragedy that when a man becomes seventeen men or twenty-seven men or forty-seven men, he does not know who is ruling at that moment, because he has no control. Obviously if he had control it should be one. When do we regain control over ourselves? When can we regulate ourselves into what we think we should be and what we really are? When all these multiple personalities become integrated into one, he is what he seems to be; and what he seems to be, is what he is.

Therefore, progress also means chipping away all these unwanted personalities within us. They fall off by cleaning; sometimes it happens like my experience which I have recounted — fear leaving me in the form of a black face exactly like my normal face; and it just moved away and it left me forever; well, it was such a bad thing in me — fear at its worst in those days.

(p.43)

The Principles of Sahaj Marg, Volume VII
Shri P. Rajagopalachari

Babuji always used to feel very sorry that people say, "Babuji! I am not progressing. I have been with you for fifteen years or twenty years, and why I am not progressing?" Babuji used to say, "The answer is obvious. Look inside yourself. Are you meditating? Are you doing the cleaning?" Sometimes he used to tell me, "Occasionally, I take the risk of asking them this question, 'How often do you meditate?' And people used to say, 'Babuji, not regularly, but at least two or three times a week!' 'Do you do the cleaning?' Many people said, 'We do not have enough time for cleaning.'" So, if you are meditating two or three times a week, and you have no time for cleaning at all, how are you going to make any progress? I suppose, only the Master can answer. Perhaps, even he could not answer, because there was no answer.

(p.1-2)

If people believe that by meditating for five minutes a day, and after that, not doing the cleaning, and then putting the whole responsibility on the Master, we can progress — yes, there may be one-in-a-million case who will progress. (p.6-7)

Babuji has told me that, in one case, he had to give as many as twenty-two sittings! Because, the first sittings are for cleaning; no transmission is given, until the person is clean enough to receive the transmission. Because, we know Babuji has said again and again, "If you transmit to a thief, he will become a perfect thief." So remove the thief from him, and then transmit to him. This took, in one case, twenty-two sittings for Master Himself! (p.11)

Many people think, that just because we meditate regularly, just because we do cleaning regularly, just because we are devoted to Master, we have a right to the goal you know, some sort of *haq* (right). I would like to disillusion you of this idea. However dedicated our practice, however sincere our approach, we have no right to the goal. It is His Grace that He gives us this. Babuji used to tell me again and again, "Only he receives to whom He wishes to give." Now, I asked Babuji, "If that is the case, then why should I practice? You do meditation, you do cleaning, you be devoted, you be obedient, you be alert, ten commandments — what is all this for?" He said, "You know the answer!" I didn't quite know it then. I took two or three days and on the third day, I got the answer during my meditation. By doing all this, in some way, we attract the Divine attention on ourselves.
(p.20-21)

— ❖ —

I told you this morning that, "Don't **think** you meditate — but **meditate**." Like in our office, we think we are working, but most of the time we are idle, talking to our neighbours, talking to our peons, going for tea and coffee, talking of election results, quietly having a radio and listening to test commentaries — is this not happening in the offices?...So, cleaning also we want like that, you see! "No, no everything Babuji does!" You see it is a very dangerous concept. It may be true, I am not prepared to dispute whether it is true or not, but it is very dangerous. It is like the rich man's son who says, "Oh! my father is there, he will help me!" — he doesn't study.

… I am sorry to note that preceptors are supporting this sort of thinking. "Everything Babuji does! What are we to do? We are nothing." Who said we are nothing? If we are nothing, we are useless even to God! Because we are something and we can be made into something, therefore He comes to help us. So we have to meditate, we have to do the cleaning. His assistance is there. It is like your telling a child, "Take up this bag." It is struggling with it, you lift it up. But if the child will not even try, you get angry with the child — "I say, you lift it." "No, no, Baba I cannot! It is so big." "Try it!"

... So if you think, "Grace is automatic, meditation He will do, cleaning He will do," then why should **I** be here at all? I need not have been born. He would have seen that I don't have to be taking birth. Don't you think so? Babuji said, "You take one step and I will not fail in taking one step." But your step is eighteen inches, His step is *saptaloka*! (all the seven worlds)

... We should, instead, be clear about the basic practice, like for instance, the way to do the cleaning. We are supposed to use our will power for cleaning. It is not just a suggestion. Can you become rich by just thinking you are rich? You have to acquire riches. Even when you have a bath, you may use the best soap, but unless you rub yourself, it will only have a superficial effect. This rubbing yourself is the will power that you use. Similarly, afterwards when you use the towel, if you just place the towel around the body and take it out, of course, it will remove some of the water, but much of it will remain. So towelling is also a brisk activity. Similarly in cleaning, you imagine, from the front, Master's Grace is sweeping through you, taking the complexities out. Babuji used to make a gesture like this, as if you are putting your hands and taking it out and throwing it aside. It is a very active, positive effort. But unfortunately people sit saying, "No, no, Babuji is cleaning me." Of course He cleans. But you know, you have to call a doctor when you are sick. The doctor doesn't go around asking, "Well, is there anybody sick here?" Isn't it? **You** have to bring him to your house. So that "bringing Him to the house" is meditation. Using Him to clean is this active process. His power you are using, but you are the user. As Babuji used to say, "Suppose I give you a knife to cut something, the power is given to you. But **you** have to cut." You just place the knife on the object and say, "O knife! Cut," will it cut? You have to use your *shakti* (power). Without the knife, you cannot cut. That knife, He gives you. But now, you want Him to bring the knife, put it on what you want to cut, cut it and say, "Here you are, take it." That is not done.   (p.41-47)

Ask for the truth and it shall be revealed to you. It cannot be denied. But ask for it sincerely, ask for it with a prayerful heart, most of all, ask for it with a heart cleared of all the mess that we have put into it. No preconceived notions, no prejudices, and say, "My Lord, my heart is now clean, please reveal." Let us try it.
(p.65)

During the meditation, I had some thoughts about the need for cleaning, systematic cleaning, daily cleaning. Surprisingly, what I thought in my mind had something to do with the total content of matter in the universe. I remember having read, a work by Fred Hoyle, that even in the outermost region of space, there is no total vacuum. His estimate was — I think it was confirmed by the Royal Society of Astrophysics or some other similar body — that even in the most far-reaching depths of space, in the outer regions of space, intergalactic space, there is one particle of matter, for two to three miles of space. Now that is hardly the level — one particle! Particle means you can't see even through electron microscopes, leave alone ordinary microscopes. What provoked this thought, I don't know, but I remember Babuji once saying about his own condition. It seems Lalaji made a remark, "Your condition is now so utterly vacuumised, that if you let anything enter into it, you will not be able to throw it out again." This is Lalaji's quotation. His Master said that his condition was so utterly vacuumised that if he was a little careless or less alert than what he should be, and allowed some thoughts to enter his system, he himself could not remove it. All of you who are concerned with engineering know how difficult it is to create vacuum. Initially yes, but a perfect vacuum cannot be achieved; even Mother Nature seems to be a failure there, if Fred Hoyle is to be believed.

That emphasizes the difficulty of thorough cleaning — number one. I was always wondering, every time I went to Master — I used to go with great eagerness, not to get something or receive something, but just to be with him — he was always very effusive in his praise for my spiritual condition, but nevertheless, on every occasion he saw me, he used to remark, "There is some grossness in you, I have to remove it." Every time — there was no exception! On one of the occasions, I had just received a letter from him before I left Madras, praising my condition so effusively, so openly, that one would have thought that I had already merged with the Infinite or some such thing. I didn't think so, but I was very happy, naturally, when my Master said, "Your condition is very much like mine. Lalaji is very pleased," and so on and so forth, you see. It so happened that fifteen days later I landed up in Shahjahanpur. He was sitting in his verandah on his easy chair. I went; he smiled first when he saw me; when I touched his feet there was a look of concentration on his face. He looked at my chest area, you see. Then he pointed and said, *"Yeh grossness hai* (this is grossness); I will have to remove it." I was a little upset and in fact, I asked him point blank in front of several abhyasis and preceptors — I said, "Babuji! Is it your failure or my failure that there is still grossness in me, as you say?" Second question: "How can I be acquiring this grossness when knowingly I have not done anything wrong, I have not thought anything wrong?" Unknowingly it might have happened, you see. He smiled and said, "Don't be worried! You know, if you have a black shirt upon you, even if a bottle of ink falls upon it, nobody will notice it. But when you have a white shirt — you are wearing a white shirt — even a spot of ink looks so blatantly dark and out of place. Your condition is so superfine, that I do not like to see even one speck of grossness on it." But I was not content that there was a speck of grossness. All right, in one way it mitigated my problem, my disappointment, but I said, "Then how could that speck come?"

Then he told something which, I think, I should reveal to you today. You know, Sahaj Marg says, samskaras are the results of our own thoughts and actions. Therefore, palpably or knowingly, if there has been no mistake of such a nature as to produce grossness, how could it come? Then he told me, "As we develop spiritually, and as our condition becomes finer and finer, we begin to act like vacuum and attract the samskaras that are around us." Babuji said, a saint is some sort of cosmic vacuum cleaner — each abhyasi has to become so. He has no choice; he cannot say, "I won't become, or I will become." Either way he has no choice. But as his condition becomes subtler, as his own inner vacuumisation proceeds, he begins to act like a small vacuum cleaner first, a larger vacuum cleaner later. Then if Master wishes and he is willing — I mean, if the abhyasi is willing and if the Master wishes — he can be a very big vacuum cleaner and then of course, inevitably, some of the dust that he takes off settles on him too. So this is one way of a sufficiently advanced person, who by himself cannot be said to be acquiring grossness by his own actions and thoughts; he can nevertheless acquire grossness from the atmosphere.

Then he told me another thing, which I sometimes hesitate to reveal because it is a very personal thing. But it is germane to our philosophy and necessary to our understanding, that we should understand that also. He said, "You are getting some grossness from your father." I said, "How is it possible?" I thought only physical characteristics could be inherited through the mechanism or the operation of the genes or chromosomes, how come even grossness can be inherited like this? He said, "Inheritance is when we are born, but this is a new finding that your case has afforded me today. I have not myself come across it so far. From your case today, I am studying that you are getting the grossness of your father." Now I was a little sad, you see, sad for my father, because knowingly or unknowingly he is passing on something to me, and unknowingly or knowingly, or even without any choice in the matter, I have to accept some of it. It is a way of nature you see, that if you are the son of your father, you get the good with the bad or the bad with the good, whichever way it is. Now, Babuji repeated it three times that day. Perhaps to assuage myself of disappointment, perhaps to bolster my falling ego, perhaps to convince me that I was not responsible for that particular grossness that I came with that day, he repeated it several times. He said, "I have examined the speck of grossness you have brought, and I am now convinced it is from your father. Of course you cannot help it, nor can he be blamed for it, but this shows how the system works, you see."

Now, there is nothing peculiar about it. If you are going to be a cosmic vacuum cleaner, or even a localised vacuum cleaner, and you can acquire the grossness of a region or a place, why not from your family too? Why should a family be distinguished and set apart? But that was not the mechanism which operated in this particular case. This was a direct sort of transfer of the father's grossness to his son. It was, of course, the first time I heard it; it was the first time Master himself discovered it. In a sense, as he told me that night — that midnight — it was the original research of his, that a father can transfer his grossness to his son and then I remembered the old biblical saying, "The sins of the father shall descend upon the son." (p.66-69)

A centre-in-charge, if he is sufficiently advanced, must take the consequences of his cleaning, a fraction of it. (p.71)

When we consider the importance of the teachings of my Master — 'grossness', we play with this word as if it is something like washing a cloth: "Take a bit of Surf, put it in water, swirl it around (like you are shown on the television) in transparent buckets, put the cloth inside, squeeze and everything is over." It is not so easy! We carry with us a burden from the past, but we carry with it also the promise of the future. Knowing this, if we are willing to live sensibly, ethically, and morally, and according to the ethics of the Master, the future is not just there, it is here — right here and now.

...It is not just superficially toying with concepts like gross-ness — "Sir, you know I went into the bus and somebody sat next to me. I felt very gross, so I did cleaning." If it was merely as superficial as that, we would have been saints the first day we came to the Master! It is like washing a doll which has become dusty. But here, it is the inside, you see. Now if you will pardon me saying it, the hatha yogi practices have tried to combat this situation, but in a very crude and superficial way. Drinking water, swerving it around your intestines by some yogic practice, ar-chaic practice — *nauti* they call it — and taking it out; *Vamana kuthi* — pulling out your intestines from behind, washing it in the river and pushing it back; it is very crude, very superficial, and not destined, not designed, to clean even the surface of the mat-ter, that is exposed to it. They knew something about it. But they could not, obviously they could not, go deeper than that. Things like *nauti, neti, pratak* — all these are very superficial. It is like washing the feet before entering the temple. Who is to wash my heart for me? Can I put a slit here (on the chest), and every time I open it, flush it with water, close up the slit and go inside? This is a sort of superficial, utterly superficial approach to cleanliness that we adopt. Even for the Brahmins, the bath is enough. If they cannot bathe, they take a fistful of water and throw it on their heads — *Imame Ganga Yamuna Saraswati* (These Ganga, Ya-muna and Saraswati) — and then say they are cleaned! All the reality was lost when the human being lost the way, forgot his Guru, gave up the practice, and had to resort to cheap trickery, ritualistic nonsense, even to live by himself. So, outside he re-mained perhaps clean, but inside he became profoundly dirty. A stage came, when those who were supposed to be clean, the cleanest of the lot, became the dirtiest of the lot.

So, the right understanding of Sahaj Marg, the right under-standing of its philosophy, the Master's teaching, is that grossness is not something like dust. I am telling you such things, from my personal sadhana, my personal experience with my Master for a period of more than twenty years. I used to be utterly disap-pointed many times, but out of that deep frustration, sense of disappointment, annoyance with the Master himself, came knowledge, came wisdom, came awakening. Because, what he could do in one sitting when I was a mere tyro in spirituality, uninitiated new abhyasi, he could not do in a hundred sittings on an advanced disciple — precisely because of the difficulties which a physicist would recognise — how to locate a particle of matter in a cubic meter of space. That was the magnitude of problem that the Master faced inside us. So it is not surprising you see, that if the abhyasis advanced, the progress is much much slower, much more delicate; the spiritual condition, the situation, much more fragile, much more subject to unintentional alterations downwards. I don't want to use the word fall. If you are for a moment not alert, you know, it is like leaving the lens of the camera open, when it is loaded with a film — the entire film is gone. Only one exposure, but the whole film is gone. So if we are less than alert, when we succumb to the pulls and pressures of the outside and the inside, what you call temptations, a whole life-time's sadhana can be destroyed in a moment, not because of any sin that we commit — in Sahaj Marg we don't have a concept of sin and virtue. Is it wrong, for instance, to associate with a girl, people ask. No. What is wrong in it? Because Babuji himself has said, that God was not a fool to create two sexes, if one is enough. But did he create two sexes for us to fool around with each other, or to dally with each other? He created for a purpose — procreation. So, when we treat it as an indulgence, the mind becomes involved; impressions are formed; the impression becomes a samskara, grossness; it hardens rock-like, cleaning becomes impossible. So there is no concept of sin, you see. There is no wrong doing and right doing in Sahaj Marg. Anything which leaves an impression is a samskara, a potential samskara and therefore a menace for spiritual development.

So, we have to be extremely alert, brothers and sisters, that we just don't fool around with spiritual sadhana, as if we have located a cinema. I know specially, you will excuse me for saying it, especially Telugu boys you see, who come to us, they go to these rotten pictures, lascivious pictures, which are only produced to inflame the lower tendencies of the human being. Next morning he is at my door, "Sir, please clean." You come at six o'clock, asking for a cleaning? Last night I saw a picture Sir, till two o'clock at night. Now I have acquired grossness. Please clean me up! So you see — just looking at a picture! If you look with absorption at what is going on, you know, it is in some way a vicarious involvement in the situation.   (p.72-76)

The concepts may be differently named, the methods to remove the grossness or weaknesses may have been utterly superficial and degraded sometimes, not because they do not know what to do, but they do not know how to do it. If the greatness of my Master lies in anything, it is not in discovering this idea of grossness, it is in his discovery of how to remove it — once and for all — and make possible in the human being's present existence, present life, evolution from whatever he may be, to the highest goal that it promises. This is the promise of Sahaj Marg and may my Master bless all of us to achieve that goal.   (p.84)

We have to work with the past in removing samskaras by cleaning, with the present in serving humanity as it is today and accepting anybody who comes, working with them make the foundation for the future that is dear to me. So, spiritual work is not just concerned with today's humanity, but past humanity, present humanity and future humanity.   (p.154)

The highest spiritual blessings, the highest spiritual grace, the highest spiritual elevation, evolution — these are reserved for them on whom His gaze falls. And how to attract that? Only through love. You see the way of sadhana is love. All this talk of meditation, cleaning — yes, initially you have to do it, but unless in your heart, love for the Master can be created, our sadhana will remain a mere exercise in self-control, perhaps a degree of self-control, a degree of self-regulation towards some higher purpose than ordinary, merely human purpose. (p.166)

Spirituality is a way not of making people go into the Central Region, but as Babuji said, to make Masters. To be a Master means to take on the responsibility, perhaps, of the whole universe itself. Such of those who are willing to undertake this tremendous responsibility, the work, they are the true abhyasis of the Master. They may not become; it is in His hands you see, but are we willing, are we ready for it? It is to create this willingness and this readiness that all this sadhana is being practised, all the books are being read, all the meditation that we do, the cleaning that we do. The lesser objectives of liberation, realisation — forget it. (p.193)

There was ever present in him, not the consciousness of his own success or failure, not even the consciousness of his existence or non-existence but that he would have to account to Lalaji, if Lalaji asked for an account — "This man has come to you for a sitting, he is still there, where he was fifteen years ago, what have you done?" Of course, the answer is obvious. "The abhyasi is not co-operating. I am cleaning him, he is adding grossness. What can I do Master?" Lalaji says, "You have the power of the Almighty with you; I am with you. I have promised you that I shall not go to the Brighter World till you are there with me. Is that not sufficient for you to be, what you have to be — that is, complete the work, that I have entrusted to you."
(p.202)

The Principles of Sahaj Marg, Volume VIII
Shri P. Rajagopalachari

What is this minimum effort that we should try to maintain? Is it five minutes of sadhana every morning? Is it following one of the ten maxims? Is it just the prayer meditation? Or is it the three minutes of cleaning in the evening? "Chari saab said 'minimum.' I cannot meditate one hour, let me meditate five minutes" — that is not the minimum. The minimum is at least to keep the contact with the Master, with the heart — your heart in contact with Master's heart. If that remains unbroken, we have this miraculous experience, that without sadhana, without ten maxims, without even cleaning, the progress goes on. (p.6-7)

The secret of spiritual success, spiritual growth, spiritual achievement according to me, brothers and sisters, today — perhaps I will change my opinion again — but today it seems to me more than anything else it is obedience. Because if the practice should get us to it there are people who have practised even in Sahaj Marg, very ardently, sometimes meditating every day four or five times, one hour each time, systematic practice. Cleaning? There are people who are cleaning themselves every evening without fail. But in many cases, Babuji Himself confirmed, even their spiritual *yatra* had not begun. (p.24)

The Sahaj Margi must be prepared to suffer more than anyone else. "No, no sir, by Master's grace, I will not suffer." It is not correct. It is a lie. Many of the abhyasis ask, specially the new ones, you know — soon after they join Sahaj Marg, problems begin. In many cases you will see this. "Sir, he started meditation three months ago; his mother died." "That man started meditation two months ago; he lost his job." But it is for our good. And imagine, if we had not come to the Master, how much more we would have to suffer all that which he has cleaned off? So whenever we have problems, miseries, diseases, sickness, loss, just try to imagine how much more it would have been, except for Babuji's Grace and His cleaning. Automatically our mind will become quiet.   (p.70)

This has been the message of my Master, this is the message of Sahaj Marg. Yesterday one gentleman asked me a question: "It is all right you are all meditating. I see there are hundreds of you, thousands of you. What is it that you contribute to national problems, for instance Punjab, Sri Lanka, so many problems?" Now this is a common misconception. No doubt my Master has said that if there is a saint of calibre in the whole world, one such saint is enough, because He is able to take into Himself like a cosmic vacuum cleaner all the samskaras of the world. So in a sense we clean, but then we see the Indian modern day culture that we sweep our houses and throw the rubbish on the streets. So this cosmic vacuum cleaner, is the cosmic Master, the present day personality of the Universe, my Master Samarth Guru Shri Ram Chandraji Maharaj of Shahjahanpur. He keeps on cleaning, taking away our samskaras, but we are creating new samskaras by our thought, by our actions. We are recreating that which He is removing from us.   (p.89)

There is a third and most important aspect which we call the cleaning system, where every evening we sit as if we are going to meditate and imagine that the Master's Grace is flowing in from the front of us, washing away the day's accumulations of impressions of our acts and thoughts, (going out) from behind in the form of smoke or vapour. This is a process of, shall we say, autosuggestion but with the will backing it so that everything that we have acquired during the day — impressions, good, bad, indifferent, it does not matter — all the impressions are removed.

(p.175-176)

How can God have favourites? So when He says "Oh I like Denmark," we must take it as a momentary thing. That is like a child in a toy shop; it likes this; then it likes that; then it likes this; it likes everything! So He likes everything; He likes everybody. No hatred, gives equal opportunity to all; the same transmission to all, the same cleaning to all. If one progresses and the other progresses not, the fault must be with the abhyasis. Opportunity is given to all. (p.202)

If there are differences in us when we start Sahaj Marg, or any other thing, you see, it is because of our samskaras. Now, our cleaning system is so superbly perfect that, that difference doesn't matter at all. You see, when you go into a house, like this house for instance, or another house like our ashram, if you have to clean up, what do you do? You do the same thing. Take a bucket of water and a mop and a broom, and you are wiping it. It doesn't matter whether it is half an inch of dust on the floor or one-tenth of a millimeter of dust on the floor — the process is the same. Isn't it? So the cleaning takes care of all the differences in samskaras between people. It doesn't matter a damn whether you are the worst sinner in creation. You have the same potential for spirituality. That is the beauty of Sahaj Marg system, you see. In other systems, no. It is not possible for such a sinner to become a saint. Why? Because cleaning is not possible. They bathe and do mantras and all that nonsense, or the priest puts water on them; it has no effect. Therefore a sinner remains a sinner, and becomes a worse sinner day by day. (p.203)

Sahaj Marg, of all the systems ever known in this world, it is the one system in which parity of all the abhyasis is there. Their difference in samskaras doesn't matter; the Guru gives equal possibility to all. His attention to everyone is equal. The goal is the same. Why we should not all be going together like in a train?

Because we don't do! Most people don't do the cleaning.

"Do you do cleaning?"

"No Chari, I am very tired when I come home from work. I go to sleep."

"Okay." What can we do? (p.204)

As I often say, you see, suppose I take two hours to create a particular samskara; suppose another samskara takes thirty minutes; and a third samskara takes six hours, and suppose it took the same time to clean a samskara as it took to create it, that is, a two hour samskara takes two hours to clean it, six hours samskara needs six, you would never be anywhere. We could not possibly do it. Isn't it? It is like one of the old films I used to see — Laurel and Hardy — where they are working in a restaurant. They have no money and they are put in the washing section, you know. There is a whole stack of plates Laurel is washing and passing to Hardy. When they think it is finished another stack comes, and another, and another. But here, Nature in its immense justice and immense mercy says, "No. You may have taken a hundred thousand lives and the samskara is there of all these hundred thousand lives. But in the first sitting, in the cleaning process, it can be almost removed provided you are co-operative, and you have the Master like Babuji."

So this is the mystery in Nature, the mercy of Nature and the justice of Nature. You may take as long as you like to make a samskara; but it can be cleaned in a few sittings. Otherwise, how is it possible to develop in one life? (p.206)

I remember, when I was made a preceptor in 1967, and I had some problems with the cleaning, Babuji gave me one advice. He asked me, "How did you do it?" I boldly replied that as I was trying to clean, I found it was all breaking up into bits and pieces.

He said, "The whole thing has been ruined!" He said "Brother, you must try to put together everything. Even if you find separate spots of blackness and grossness, try to bring them together and remove them in one unit." You know, that is the common wisdom of the housewife, who sweeps, brings together all the rubbish, takes it on the broom and throws it out. Evil has to be accumulated; good has to be spread far.

... So this is a very basic wisdom, you see, like we put all evil together and destroy it together in one stroke. You have the modern electronic marvel, of something you plug in, and all the mosquitoes are destroyed. Paralleling it, there is the marvel of Master's creation when He was dealing with evil spirits some fifteen years back, and He found that, one by one He could not do anything with them. It was a tedious task, it was a laborious task, time consuming, painful. He told me He created a sort of a parabolic mirror somewhere up in the Himalayas, and it was a mirror of thought into which He put the power of thought to attract all the evil spirits and destroy them. Even today that work is going on.   (p.216-218)

The Principles of Sahaj Marg, Volume IX
Shri P. Rajagopalachari

Originally I only went for what I thought I needed. Now he is giving me things which I never knew I needed; awakening impulses in me which I don't know existed, subduing my baser tendencies, eradicating them from my system. See cleaning is only a term that we use in Sahaj Marg. What is it that He removes? Is there a removal, or is there a transformation? Because as Babuji said, "Remove hatred and there is love." Is love created? It's only a removal of hatred. Removal of hatred in what form? Because it is a thought. It is an emotion. Nevertheless strong enough, sometimes to last perhaps life after life, in an eternity of hatred that is difficult to remove. He says, "It becomes hard like, it is almost impossible to remove that grossness." See these are the miracles He does. (p.157)

If I claim to be His disciple I have to obey Him. He says, "Meditate," I meditate. "No, no, Babuji, I am your representative." He says, "Doesn't matter. You still sit and meditate." I still sit and meditate. I do my cleaning. Why not? I know Babuji used to say very often, everybody here must have heard it that He had such enormous accumulation of grossness that periodically Lalaji used to come and clean it! How can He not have grossness? It may not be His, it may be the grossness of the abhyasis that He is cleaning off, some of which comes on to Him, but nevertheless there was grossness and He needed to be cleaned. And Lalaji did it or some others did it, I don't know. He has said it jokingly, He has said it seriously. I know He has cleaned Himself very often when He got up from the chair and suddenly He would stand up and you know, and do that for a few seconds! It was cleaning Himself!

So, when the Master needs to clean Himself, when the Master's Master needs to clean the Master periodically, who are we to say we don't need cleaning? So let us stick to the principles of our Sahaj Marg system. Imagination is nice! I too wish to have all this without meditation! Even though the system is simple, we are only to meditate for half an hour and do cleaning for thirty minutes, yet it is irksome, you know. (p.197-198)

The system is something which we have to practice. For heaven's sake, don't give it up because it is Master who wants us to meditate. It is He who wants us to do our cleaning. I remember, once He wrote a very strict and rather painful letter to the then preceptor-in-charge of Hyderabad. They had sent a batch of eight or ten abhyasis to Shahjahanpur and Babuji wrote a very strict letter. He said, "You are sending me these people. I have been watching for years. You are not doing any preparation. You have not even done cleaning, so that when they come to me I have to kill myself doing the cleaning, denying them the opportunity of further advancement which should have been theirs, because they come with limited time," you see. It is like you are taking a dirty vessel to the milk booth and while everybody is waiting in the queue, you start washing your vessel. Will the milkman wait? He will say, "Why don't you bring a clean vessel for heaven's sake?" This is the preceptor's duty you see and that man was fired. It was a letter of which I have a copy even today. He said, "What are you doing? I have to do your work and I have to do my work too." Babuji has written clearly, "If I have to do the preceptor's work and my own work also, why do I need preceptors?" So you see, this is a highly technical, highly competent, highly scientific, highly precise system, I make bold to say if anybody can challenge it! And then to bring in irrational adventurism into it and say, "I got"! "Yes, I too have got," but it is the benefit of *sadhana*, not without *sadhana*.   (p.200)

Then comes the process of purification when we can say, "Nothing *in* me now governs my action or my thought." It is original thought in the sense that I am now thinking for myself. I am not just throwing up something from inside, you see. It is very correct when, intuitively, we use the phrase, "He is just vomiting what he has read."

...All our thoughts are like that, all our actions are like that. We vomit and therefore very often it is nauseating even to ourselves! Therefore yoga says, "All that you have brought, yes, it is something you did, that you thought, which created this pattern." After all, when you record something on a cassette, it is you who have recorded it, you have to erase it. Some assistance is given by the mechanism which is provided for it. You cannot possibly do it by erasing with your fingers like we can erase the blackboard.

So go to one who is able to do these things for you. Erase what is already written, like changing a computer program. It has immense possibilities. Its capacity is unlimited, that of the mind.
(p.229-230)

The Principles of Sahaj Marg, Volume X
Shri P. Rajagopalachari

I have one request to make. My Master Babuji Maharaj was often pointing out to us that people used to come to him for three days, ten days, fifteen days, often for Basant, and they would go sight-seeing afterwards on their way home. So he used to say, "Look here, what foolishness they are committing. They come here, I clean them, purify them, fill them and when they go home they should go home straight. Instead of that they are going sight-seeing, they are going to Patna, they are going to Kathmandu and to Benares and they are spoiling their condition even before they reach home. Please tell them that at least if they want to do all these foolish things, they should do it before they come here, so that I can clean them and they go home clean."

So, I have to make that request to you all over again, that if you want to do any sight-seeing, do it tomorrow, so that afterwards we don't allow our thoughts to stray hither and thither. Because though Babuji Maharaj has said, constant remembrance is the simplest thing in the world, and has said that if you are able to do it for one week, you cannot stop doing it afterwards, it's not possible. When we are away from here or wherever the celebrations are being held — what we call temporarily the centre — we know how difficult it is to think of the Master, remember Him, think of meditation, do the cleaning. But sometimes I feel it is even more difficult when we are there with Him. Because in some way, we think, we are at the centre now, we can afford to go elsewhere. "After all, we are with the Master, what does it matter if I go for two hours somewhere and come back?" It is like a man saying, "After all, I am clean, I just had a bath. Why shouldn't I get into the gutter for half an hour and come out again?"   (p.51)

Many people ask why should I have to meditate all my life, day in and day out. It is monotonous, it is nauseating sometimes, cleaning over and over again, every day. What is this grossness that cannot be got rid of at one stroke? If Babuji Maharaj is such a great personality (next comes this question) how is it that he could not, as he himself said, create a few hundred saints in Sahaj Marg? I remember he told Dr. K.C. Varadachari way back in 1966-67, "For all the effort I have been putting in upon South India, I should have had at least a hundred personalities in the South alone." Not one or two — a hundred. "But," he added, "I haven't been able to create one yet."   (p.58-59)

Strangely enough, at the same time, Babuji said that his work on human beings is a very small fraction of this total work. He also said it is the most difficult, because for him to clean the cosmos was the work of a second. He just looked at the cosmos and it was clean. When the sun shines, it doesn't make sure that before it goes to a dark place, somebody carries a lamp to illuminate the way. It shines and there is light. God looks and there is cleanliness. God laughs and the whole world laughs. God is happy and the world is happy. It is we who need lanterns to take us into the darkness.   (p.96)

You can polish your silver once a month but, your toilet has to be cleaned every time you use it. Into that gutter he descends again and again and we keep spoiling it, polluting it.

That is why he needed preceptors. Of course, Babuji has told me hundred times, "Really speaking I don't need preceptors," and I have asked him because my ego was hurt — I am a preceptor and he says, "I don't need preceptors." What the hell is going on here? And I asked him, "How come, why do you make us preceptors?" I at least didn't know what was happening to me when I was made a preceptor. I am like a bird which is caught and put into a cage. I had never any choice. He said, "I need you to do the cleaning because, I can do it, of course, but face to face the cleaning is perfect. You must evaluate the condition, you must study the grossness, remove it. All this is not possible, sitting at a distance. Therefore I have preceptors."

Therefore it is said that most of the preceptor's work for most of this life is only cleaning, but it is always a nice piece of fantasy to think that you are elevating people. Everybody likes to elevate people but not to clean them. Cleaning is a dirty job — a strictly Indian way of looking at work. Cleaning is difficult, there is no question about it, if you really do your job as preceptors.   (p.97)

See, this is basically, essentially, overall, a system of **being**. And to be something, you have to become that which you have to be.

The process of becoming is our Sahaj Marg way: the meditation, the cleaning, the night prayer. Only to become that which the Master cherishes and loves so much that He cannot be away from us.   (p.136)

...You cannot taint the Divine. You cannot taint the untaintable. You cannot sully the unsulliable. You cannot dirty that which is ever cleaning us.   (p.142)

It is a very simple system. It hinges around mainly three aspects of sadhana: (i) meditation, (ii) the cleaning process in the evening, and (iii) a prayer at night-time. (p.186)

There is no way of changing the past. But does it mean we are slaves of the past? My Master said, "No." Because of the cleaning system that he has evolved, it removes, by his grace, by his mercy, by his compassion, all the impressions of thoughts and actions that we have built in ourselves. (p.192)

In Sahaj Marg, while the guru demands a certain degree of *bhoga* of samskara for our good as a self-educational process, the bulk of it is removed by this cleaning process. It is like erasing a slate of the child. It is now cleaned; you start again.

My Master used to say that even in one sitting of his transmission and this cleaning process, the samskaras of several lives are gone. Not just one life in which you remove just one samskara, several lives. Imagine! I have been myself almost now thirty years in this *marg* starting as his disciple, and life goes on. I am sometimes horrified to see the extent of samskaric burden I must have brought into this existence that, day after day, day after day, this cleaning is going on. (p.199)

Therefore the *sadhakas* (the abhyasis, as we call them) have to be alert that they do not do something to bring on themselves a further load of samskaras. Otherwise it is like somebody is washing the floor and somebody is going on spitting behind him.

We have many myths. You know the myth of Sisyphus, for instance, where there is eternally this thing going on: climbing up four feet, climbing back four feet, climbing up four feet, climbing back four feet, eternally going on. So the cleaning process of

Sahaj Marg system is absolutely, inexorably effective. But that is not the end of the system. We have to co-operate, in not doing something, in not thinking something.

Remember, thought is more potent. That is why in the *sandhyavandana kriya* we have to start with "*manasa vacha hastabhyam*" (Through mind, speech and hands.) The mind is the originator of everything. My Master used to say, "The mind is our enemy, but the mind is also a friend." You have to regulate the mind to be a friend, remove its effects, *vasanas*, clean off the samskaras. (p.200)

In the evening we have this process of cleaning, as I told you. We are taught to imagine that all the samskaras which are seated in the heart are going from behind like smoke or vapour. And we can actually feel lighter at the end of this process. (p.203)

The inner life, the life of the transcendental self, has no limits. That is why we say spirituality is capable of taking you to the ultimate stage which we call divinisation. But there too it is by driblets of energy put upon ourselves: sitting in meditation for an hour, doing the cleaning in the evening for half an hour, prayer at night for ten minutes. Brick by brick by brick we build our spiritual destiny, unfailing destiny which cannot be ever limited, which cannot be stopped by anybody except ourselves. (p.240)

We must be able to do our daily sadhana, especially the cleaning in the evening, do it systematically, do it with dedication, do it with a sense of purpose that, "I have to remove from my system those things which are doing harm to me, which are sort of blocking my path." I hear many people come up and tell me, "Sir, even during cleaning I have these thoughts." Of course, when you bathe, the water flowing off your body will be a little dirtier than the water which flows on to you. But wait till clean water flows off you. That is the time to stop your bath.   (p.251)

Make up your minds that the day shall not break without my meditating, the sun shall not set without my cleaning and I shall not go to bed without my prayer-meditation. The rest will take care of itself.   (p.255)

The Role of the Master in Human Evolution
Shri P. Rajagopalachari

So this is the real connection between the abhyasi and the guru, you see. He seeds, we provide the soil; and like any soil, it must be kept clean, free of insects, free of weeds, we have also to co-operate in this cleaning of ourselves. Otherwise it becomes like the grass, you see, a mixture of everything, weeds, nettles, grass. So that also makes another feeling grow in us that we have to co-operate. So these are the elements of his teaching. He seeds, we allow it to grow within us, and we find the evidence for this growth in the very teaching that he provides for us.   (p.39)

So I said, "Babuji, but can you not tell me now what you were doing?" So, he put on one of his famous smiles and gave me the answer, he said, "I was doing the same thing I am doing all the time." That made me no wiser and made me understand nothing more than I had understood a little earlier. So I said, "Babuji, what was that?" He said, "Transmitting!" as if it was such an easy thing, I should have known it long ago. Then I said, "Babuji, transmitting again?" He said, "Well, I am telling you, there are only two things we have to do: clean and transmit." So that was interstellar work, cosmic work, whatever you like to call it. So this gave me a further expansion in my concept, in my mental concept that our work in spirituality expands beyond the human beings to other worlds, whatever they may be.   (p.47)

The second thing concerns the cleaning, and I have already, I think, touched upon it in the talk given yesterday morning. Because, as I have tried to explain to you, we come into this world with our load of samskaras, which is our own creation. And that is the capital we bring into this existence. It continues to guide our lives totally. Though we enjoy a spurious or false sense of freedom (spurious can also be taken as a limitation, you see), like you have a Sony recorder, if somebody makes another one and puts on the Sony label, it is spurious. So whatever we may think about our own freedom, we are not really free, and we can be free only when our samskaras are erased, which is achieved by the cleaning process. My Master once clarified the utmost importance of not continuing to form samskaras. It should have been a very easy thing that we bring some samskaras into this existence, and they are removed off by a graceful Master. But every time we think something or do something, there is the possibility of creating another impression or a samskara. Therefore spiritual success, or success in spiritual life, does not depend only on the meditation and the cleaning. If you are going to add on samskaras day by day, the cleaning process becomes endless, and therefore the meditation cannot be really effective.   (p.99)

Similarly, it is the weight of our past which is holding us down. And I may say with absolute confidence that the cleaning aspect of Sahaj Marg alone is sufficient to give us most of the blessings of spiritual practice, since ninety percent of our deficiencies, of our drawbacks of the gravitational hold of samskaras is released in one stroke.

This, I consider, is something unique to Sahaj Marg. Though the idea of cleaning is not foreign to even religious systems, it has remained a superficial approach to physical cleansing and, perhaps, to psychic cleaning process — to my knowledge nothing more than that, nothing deeper than that. And therefore all temple rituals, church rituals, have remained merely rituals. That is why when we go there and come out, we don't feel a sense of either elation or lightness or joy, which almost without exception every abhyasi feels after the cleaning process. I hope you have all experienced this.

So that is the fantastic difference between the rituals of religion and the spiritual cleaning process as given by my Master: this buoyancy, this feeling of lightness; and that is why in a sense Babuji says, "We don't see light, but we feel light." And how does this feeling of lightness come? Precisely because the weight of samskaras is removed; I therefore repeat, it achieves ninety percent of what we have to achieve under spiritual practice. Whenever we meet abhyasis anywhere in the world, and we find that they are not progressing, almost invariably it is because they have not done the cleaning.

Now Babuji Maharaj has said, if you receive transmission while your tendencies are still active, only those tendencies will be strengthened. As he puts it very pithily, "If you transmit to a thief, he will become a perfect thief." That is why I have always felt that transmission without cleaning cannot achieve much, or at least it cannot achieve much in the direction we want it to achieve. Therefore I have emphasized the fundamental requirement, the most important requirement of our sadhanas, the cleaning process. Therefore we also advise abhyasis: whenever you cannot meditate, at least do the evening cleaning, because it keeps the vessel pure to receive the transmission. So this is the very great benefit of the cleaning process, and whatever else we may neglect, the cleaning should not be neglected under any circumstances.   (p.101-103)

So I would like to close this rather lengthy discourse on the Master with an effort to recall to you his single requirement of spirituality — a fundamental requirement — through all necessary things, whether it be material things, habits, mental things: be simple and in tune with nature, and cultivate the habits he cultivated and showed us. Because, as he once told me himself from yet another example in his life, he never meditated for more than two or three minutes at a time. He also told me that he rarely did the cleaning. And he was often troubled in his conscience that he was not able to do these things. But one day, he said, when he was going to brush his teeth — he was walking to the well in his house, a matter of five metres — his heart was breaking with an anguish to be like his Master, and the thought came into his mind, "I must be like my Master." It was not just a thought, it was an anguished cry from his heart, backed by all the tremendous and profound love for his Master. And then Lalaji's voice came, "You are like me now."

So, in the final analysis, it is not the practice, it is not meditation, it is not cleaning, though of course they are all necessary. But it is not these that give us the final success. They may give us petty things like liberation, childish things, but if we want that which he got, we must create in ourselves that hunger, that longing, that absolute need, to love him in such a way that we want to become like him. (p.110)

In spirituality we have nothing but the truth, the whole truth. Because the Master exists, we sit before him, we receive or do not receive, as we experience it among ourselves, by our growth. And like when you put clothes out to dry, it takes half an hour, one hour, two hours, depending on how wet the cloth is. Similarly depending on our level of grossness, a certain time is taken, before we can know what we are getting. Therefore it is necessary to have patience until we are relatively dry in his presence, that is, so that we are at least relatively clean. I was using the word 'dry' because of the cloth, you see. It is like a window-pane. If it is very dirty you cannot see through it. It does not mean there is no light outside. So we have to clean it until it allows the light to come inside. This cleaning, too, is largely done by the Master.

(p.126)

And Babuji adds the very, very important advice that if you go on dwelling on your guilt, you are deepening the impressions of what you have already done and making stronger and stronger samskaras. So, Babuji says, "Repent for what you have done." And a true repentance consists not in saying "I repent! I repent!" a thousand times, but in determining once and for all not to commit the mistakes again. And what about removing the effects of the thing we have done? That is taken care of in the cleaning. So, in our system of Sahaj Marg, we have a very healthy way of handling guilt, and it is not only healthy, it is the most effective.

(p.159)

But when we come to Sahaj Marg, and we are taught and we believe and we accept the teaching that it is our samskaras which make us responsible for our existence, then we have to face the blame very squarely for the first time ourselves. Therefore, the feelings of guilt are much more terrible in a spiritual system. Why? Because we cannot possibly run away from ourselves. It is easy to run away from the home or from the church or even from your country, but where can you run away from yourself?

So, that is as far as the situation is concerned. How to change it? We know very well, you see. Do the cleaning better, forget the feeling of guilt and deposit even that feeling with the Master.

(p.160)

The word creation being used in its widest possible sense, that is, as representing the entire universe, manifested and unmanifested universe. And Sahaj Marg and my Master, they teach us that therefore, love is very necessary, but it has to be guided in the right direction. And this is what we are trying to do in meditation, constant remembrance, cleaning and all these things.

(p.168-169)

As far as anger is concerned, what is the need for it? Master's answer was that anger in its pure sense, not to be confused with rage or other violent ways of expression, I can't find the right words for it — it provides what can be considered the motor-force in cleaning up all that is wrong. That is, in its pure form, anger functions against all ungodly manifestations in nature. So anger should not be used against each other for destructive purpose, or things like that.

(p.169)

The Fruit of the Tree
Shri P. Rajagopalachari

Q: After the cleaning it is not possible for me to sleep. Why such a vitality which could make me do another day of work?

A: After cleaning?

Q: After cleaning.

A: I wish I had it. (laughter)

There seem to be quite some points of departure from recommended practice as far as cleaning is concerned. In fact Pia referred to the fact that it was a suggestion that she should meditate before supper, but it is not correct. Babuji's system says, do the cleaning when your day's work is over. For men it means when they come back from their work. They should have a wash, and sit and do their cleaning. For women, well, if they are cooking they should finish the cooking, or if they are working girls, they should come back from work and the same thing applies to them. So that is number one. We should do the cleaning according to the time that is set for it, that is, when the day's work is over. Now what do we do in cleaning? That is important, because I find that many people meditate instead of cleaning themselves. All of you should carefully read the one sheet of paper we used to give in Shahjahanpur, *Practice for Beginners*. It says, sit as if you are going to meditate. I mean, the pose is the same as you would adopt for the meditation.

... the grossness is cleaned out of us by something which is entering from in the front and taking it out of the back in the form of smoke or vapour.

Here I want to emphasize something which I found many people haven't understood, that in the cleaning process one has to apply one's will. In meditation we don't apply our will at all. In meditation it's a question of fixing our attention on the object on which we are meditating. Now this is perhaps why many people find that instead of doing the cleaning they're meditating, because if the will is not applied, it becomes something of a farce. But because we sit in the aspect of meditation, in the attitude, or in the posture we normally adopt, the mind having become used to meditation, it slips into meditation. So my Master, Babuji, used to always emphasize that when we sit for cleaning, we should apply the will. And He used to make a gesture, you know, as if you are putting your hand into your heart and throwing out things, like this, from behind. That is the correct way of doing the cleaning; and the right time, as I have said earlier, is when the day's work is over.   (p.8-9)

Now that is a good thing, that the energy is at least coming out during the cleaning, because the purpose of cleaning is to remove everything which is unnecessary, and if there we have unnecessary power, that should also go. And if that is correct, then this should not continue forever. Because after cleaning there is always a sense of normal, natural well-being. Nothing ecstatic, nothing joyful, but shall we say, a state of contentment; and that makes it possible for us to go to sleep in a very harmonious way. In fact, the whole idea — I mean the idea of giving this system of cleaning to be done at that particular time, after the day's work is over — is to remove all the heaviness, both by way of grossness and by way of mental tensions, that we have accumulated, and put us into a harmonious mood. So that even our dinner we can eat in peace, digest it in a normal way, and then go to sleep in a very harmonious way. So that is why it is important to do it at the right time, when the day's work is over.

Q: Should we remember every event of the day?

A: No, no.

This lady asked a question whether she should remember every event of the day and try to clear its impressions. But when we have a bath do we remember every dirty thing that we touched and try to clean it away? It's a general thing you see.

I may perhaps also tell you the importance of doing the meditation at the right time. Since we have talked about the cleaning, we might as well talk of the meditation. Because the cleaning prepares the system in one way, the meditation fulfills our spiritual requirements in another way. The whole problem comes because some people say, "Well I cannot meditate at such and such a time, can I do it later?" So we say, well, you are not able to do the cleaning in the evening because you come at nine o'clock, then you're too tired to do the meditation, combine both before you go to bed. But this is an exception for one or two occasions when you're really tired, but people begin to adopt it as a continuous thing all the year round because it suits them. I have never found that any serious abhyasi had any problem about doing the meditation at the specified time or the cleaning at the specified time. So it only means that until our interest in our own spiritual development is established, we have these problems.

People talk of sacrifice, but it is my personal view that the whole idea of sacrifice is a mistake; it's a wrong thing. Because when we have two interests, let us say social existence and spiritual existence, then comes the question of choosing between the two. Now what happens, even there it is not a sacrifice. Suppose one day you choose to do the cleaning instead of meeting your friend and the next day you choose to meet your friend instead of doing the cleaning; it is a natural acceptance of the idea that you can do only one thing at a time.   (p.10-11)

Q: Once I was alone in the meditation hall and I had fear about the picture of Lalaji.

A: Lalaji. Yes. I'm happy I'm not the only one. (laughter) So why this fear of Lalaji? It only shows there is some fear in us which reacts to certain things outside. Somebody is afraid of dogs, somebody is afraid of snakes, somebody is afraid of the darkness, somebody is afraid of noises. What we are afraid of depends on the samskaras we carry inside us. Therefore when this cleaning is finished you cannot have fear any more. Therefore saints are fearless. They will go in the jungle, you know, the elephant comes, the lion goes with them, the tiger walks in front of them, they have no fear. How can they be afraid? — there is no samskara here. Therefore, when you become fearless, it means nothing here. No temptation, because temptation is also like that — from the heart. If temptation is in the thing, all should be tempted by it. But it is here, so I am tempted by something by which you are not tempted. Temptation is not outside, it is inside. So temptation, fear, everything must go when cleaning is complete.
(p.69-70)

You see, surrender is not a process, like cleaning is a process, meditation is a process. Now in cleaning we are doing something to remove something, to achieve a different condition.   (p.71)

I feel a sensation which tells me that my stomach is empty and I need something put into it. Similarly with thirst. My body needs fluids, drink—it doesn't mean I should take wine or beer. It means my body needs some fluid content. Similarly, when I feel unclean, I take a bath. Now there's no word for clean and unclean. You can only say, "I feel dirty." This is external dirt, which you can see, you can touch and say, "Oh, it's all black." Internal dirt, grossness, we don't feel. So the Master comes and says, you are gross, do the cleaning. Now you need outside help. So first we depend on ourselves — we feel hungry, we feel thirsty, we feel sick, we feel happy, all these things and we try to fulfil these needs ourselves.

Then come the inner needs: that I am heartbroken, I have to go to the psychiatrist; I have bad dreams, I have to go to somebody else. Now I need God. I cannot find Him, I don't know where He exists or how to get in touch with Him, so I go to the Master and He says, "All right, first do the cleaning and then take the sitting." (p.72)

Q: The last question: "Some evenings, when I have very little time, I do a cleaning of ten or fifteen minutes only. Is this sufficient, is it efficacious?"

A: You answer it. (to an abhyasi)

Abhyasi: Master says that the cleaning process in the evening must be of twenty minutes up to half an hour, but independently of the time of cleaning I think that unless the feeling of lightness and calmness and of the removal of grossness has developed in the abhyasi during the cleaning, he must not stop until this condition has been acquired. So half an hour is necessary I think. Is it right?

A: The whole thing is a question of following what is prescribed by the Master. You know, we have, sometimes, people who go to a doctor and he gives them a big bottle of medicine — sixteen doses of medicine to be taken three times a day, one in the morning, one in the afternoon, one at night, for five or six days. Now if the man imagines that by drinking all of it at one stroke, he can be well sooner, we might have a dead man. So we must leave to the doctor to tell us what we should do, how much we should do, when we should do it, and follow it. We must remember that, because something is good, more of the same thing will not be better, and some more will not be the best. This is why we get drunk and things like that. One glass of wine is good, a second glass of wine makes me a little giddy, the third one—I'm out (he chuckles), out for the count. So even good things need not be good by having more of them. That's why we have a saying in Tamil, I think I told you before, that even nectar, which is supposed to give you immortality, must be taken in limited doses.

Abhyasi: So it is not right to wait for the feeling of lightness? Well, I gave a wrong answer. (laughter)

A: (He laughs) Because, you see, I have a shirt, normally I wash it and it is clean. But suppose I have put ink in it, very black ink, if I go on washing until I clean it, I will tear the cloth. So I have to wash it a little, normal wash, there is still some ink, wear it two days then wash it again, some more ink goes. It takes maybe six or seven washes, you see, I cannot do it in one wash. So if I try to wash in one wash, I don't have the shirt. So that is why our cleaning process says, when the abhyasi does the cleaning it is to remove the impressions of the day, accumulated during the day. The past impressions are the work of the preceptor and the Master.

(p.74-75)

Heart to Heart, Volume I
Shri P. Rajagopalachari

Q: In *Efficacy of Raja Yoga,* I think Babuji speaks of cleaning through point B, to reduce sensuality. Can you explain this technique?

A: It is to be undertaken only when the Master advises it. Otherwise you do your regular cleaning as we are always doing it. The points A and B are essentially for preceptors to work upon. Unless the abhyasi is advised to do this technique, it should be avoided. (p.119-120)

Well, one has to exorcise the devil. How to do it? As he very nicely said, "Go into it and bring it out." So here we have the superficial self, the 'I' in me; I have my own internal self, the He in me; and I have the negative part of myself, the dark half, the devil in me. God and devil cannot fight, because the devil will never fight God. But within me there is God, luring me inside myself. The devil who is trying to tempt me to do things which I shouldn't. Therefore, essentially, the 'I', the superficial 'I', has to enter the war. Then we find that the He in me supports the 'I' in me, and the devil is exorcised. And in this process, especially in Sahaj Marg, the Master's help is there by helping us to exorcise the devil by the cleaning process, and by adding the transmission, which strengthens the He in me, and by the simplicity that is introduced in us which progressively eliminates the 'I'. So that essentially, finally, the He in me is warring the devil in me, and that's a very successful battle. (p.297-298)

Now, normally preceptors are expected to do cleaning. If you devote thirty minutes to a sitting, you give twenty-five minutes attention to cleaning and only last five minutes to transmission. Because transmission is such an immense thing. It's like washing out a vessel. You have had something in it. You want to clean it and get the milk. The cleaning takes more time. Pouring the milk into it hardly takes any time. You open a tap and it's full. So transmission need not be given for more than a few minutes.

(p.338)

I cleaned the glass chimney of my lamp so that it should not block the light that was burning from the flame. Isn't it? Similarly the system of the abhyasis cleaned by the Master not for his sake but so that the Divine flame inside may be visible to all. Which means that this Divine flame is to illuminate others, show them the way, not just for itself and rest in an easy chair. So it is not only the Master and the preceptors who have to work, every abhyasi must become an illuminant — illuminator, you see, a lamp. That's what the biblical statement means, "Hide not thy lamp under a bushel."   (p.348-349)

Heart to Heart, Volume II
Shri P. Rajagopalachari

So, what he removed by the cleaning was the compulsive effect of the past on us, and substituted it by himself, a person whom we love, whom we adore, whom we revere. What is the result? That when we worked because of our samskaras, we hated our work, it was a bondage, but when we work for one whom we love, whom we adore, it becomes a pleasure.   (p.45)

In fact, when I first asked Babuji, "What is the purpose of these three or four sittings that you give to new abhyasis?" he said, "It is to clean." I said, "Clean what?" The standard answer, "Grossness." I asked him, "Why, cleaning of the grossness?" Then he told me it is like one of these oil lamps in the past, which had a glass chimney. It had become coated with black soot, so thick that the light could not come outside.

In a similar fashion with our grossness we have completely enclosed the Divine Light burning in our hearts. And even though the Light is inside us, we cannot see it, we cannot perceive it, we cannot even feel it. Babuji added, "If I ask you to meditate and you cannot see the light, though it is not a visible light that I expect you to see, nevertheless, if there is a barrier between it and yourself, it will block your efforts at meditation. Therefore I have to clean it sufficiently for you to be able to perceive the reality hidden in your heart." So this is what is done during the first three or four sittings... (p.53-54)

Very often I have found in the time of my Master and now, it is the people who don't meditate who want to know how to meditate. It is the people who don't clean themselves who are worried about blockages, grossness. ...

So practical questions can be answered by doing things for you and showing how it is to be done. That is what the Master does. He delays the answer, gives you the time to meditate, does a little cleaning and removes the question from your mind. (p.62)

And if you look at your heart and you find hatred in it, that will be your future, unless you remove it. Now if you clean a fossil of the past, you do not remove anything, you only have a clean fossil, it is still very much dead. But if you look into your heart and you find hatred there, and you know that if you leave it there, your future is going to be one of hatred and nothing else. You realise the need, very vital need, for cleaning. You look into your heart and you find wrong tendencies, you know what is your future, wrong tendencies, wrong actions, wrong results.

And if you look in your heart and find Him, that too is your future, that is what I am going to become. So, the spiritual science of my Master says, "Look into the heart, meditate on the light in the heart which is eternally present there, do the cleaning, so that all unnecessary things are removed, which too are only impressions of the past." ... These fossils in our heart, our samskaras, tell us what to remove and what shall be the future.

So you see the enormous difference of looking into the past and looking into the future, looking into the material universe and looking into the inner universe of the heart. Therefore, when we find hatred, viciousness, corruption, disease forms, we know these are things which are going to govern our future, unless they are taken out. Therefore, we are advised to do the cleaning, and the Master, in his enormous mercy for us, cleans off the immense burden of samskaras which we cannot possibly remove. (p.88-89)

Q: About the cleaning. Should the smoke be evacuated through the back or through the backbone?

A: There is no smoke. We are asked to imagine that the grossness is going out like smoke from the whole back. Otherwise we would have drilled a hole and put a tube for it to go out (laughter). (p.153)

Q: Why this fear, this incapacity to communicate? What to do so that I wouldn't be afraid anymore, but especially for not being aggressive and nervous?

A: More cleaning. (p.154)

Q: How to do one's cleaning well? Should we do it before we go to bed, or a little bit before in the evening?

A: If we start doing it, we will do it well. I do not know what is the difference between cleaning and cleaning well. If I go for a bath, can I come out without bathing well? The same thing for cleaning. Do it, and it is done well. The instructions are clear, do it after the day's work is done. Only if it is not possible on certain occasions, we should do it at bed time. And not possible means really not possible. Most of these 'not possibles' are imaginary.
(p.156)

...we have the samskaras of the past some of them we have to undergo. Even though ninety percent, ninety-eight percent is removed by cleaning.   (p.170)

True action only comes when there are no samskaras, or very little samskaras. Then you are acting in a real sense. **you** are acting, not your samskaras. You see, like when a body is in motion, and the force is withdrawn from it, if there's no resistance it will move forever. You know about Newton's laws—a body in motion will continue to be in motion. What is it that keeps it in motion? The moment of inertia. Isn't it? Similarly, we are kept going through life after life by this moment of inertia, which is produced by our samskara. How can you say he is responsible for it? He is responsible in the sense he created the moment of inertia for himself. So the responsibility for stopping it is also given to you. Clean yourself.   (p.262-263)

In Sahaj Marg, a samskara is formed by an action or a thought. And all samskaras, *per se*, are undesirable. So we don't have this distinction between good samskara and bad samskara. The intention is to avoid formation of samskaras if possible. And my Master says it is possible because by cleaning we get rid of past samskaras and by proper living, it is possible to lead life without forming fresh samskaras. That is our goal, I mean goal of life, not the goal of meditation.   (p.314)

Heart to Heart, Volume III
Shri P. Rajagopalachari

But the point is, how did I come to this understanding that a master must love without judgement? Through my practice, because when you look inside yourself in meditation, inevitably you find all the ugly things, the dirty things, the stupid things inside. There have been occasions, during meditations, when I have had so much nausea that I have had to vomit physically. I was nauseated with myself. Now when you are exposed to your inner condition, you see, outside you can clean and, you know, polish and paint. What about **this** inside here?   (p.39)

As I said in the beginning, "We are not taught not to judge, so that we should not be judged." But we come to the realisation that there is nothing to judge. Because inside me there is nothing, though there is the whole universe itself. Now when there is nothing in me, we do not call it nothing, we call it nothingness. Who is the judge? Who is to be judged and what is to be judged? And such a person sees the same thing in everybody, because the reality inside the heart of every person in the universe is the same. Then what is this all about? You can ask, "Why this lecture? Why this talk? Why this yoga business?" Because it is like something which is covered up, like a lamp with dirty glass around it. Clean it and the light is the same. So the whole thing is nothing, you know, we do not become pure. My Master's teaching does not recognize anything as pure or impure. It only says there is an original condition which we have covered over by our activities and our thoughts. Remove this and then you expose the inner reality, which was always there.   (p.48)

And here the grace of the guru, or the Master, is necessary, because however much we may use the mind, and however we may perfect it, if the human tendencies we have brought into this birth are not changed, then the mind continues to work in the same way as before, only more powerfully now. So one of the fundamental techniques of Sahaj Marg, perhaps the most important, is what we call cleaning.   (p.56)

Now Fausto Russo talked something about cleaning. That is a very important aspect of our yogic tradition. Because my Master's research indicates that whenever we think or do something, it leaves an impression on the mind. And when these impressions are repeated, again and again, they become hard, and what we call 'grossness' comes into being. And unless they are removed, whatever we may do, we cannot be pure. Pure, not in the sense in which it is understood today, you see, cleanliness, truth, and things like that, but spiritually pure, that is, subtle. Because my Master's teaching was, "God is the subtlest thing in existence," so subtle that we can hardly say He exists; whereas we are at the physical end of the spectrum where it is totally gross. What we have to do, by this system of cleaning, is to remove this grossness progressively, become subtler and subtler until we have achieved that level of subtlety which is **His**. And then only union can happen, you see.

...So in that sense, there was nothing wonderful about what my Master had revealed. There was nothing esoteric, nothing occult. It was a very simple teaching. Until you shed your grossness and become subtle like Him, you cannot mix with Him. Not in the sense of intermingling with Him, union with Him.

So that is why our cleaning method is the most important aspect of the Sahaj Marg practice. It emphasizes the need to participate in it, every evening, as a discipline. This is very effective. And the Master helps by periodically cleaning us to the extent of the need to do the practice of meditation. And, as we become progressively subtler and subtler, even our living habits change.

(p.110-112)

And here you see the great lesson of spirituality, that as long as you remember yourself, you are conscious of your existence, the need to be healthy, happy and wise, and the need to be safe and secure. Think of Him, all is forgotten. So you see, real safety, real health, real security, comes only by remembrance of the

Master. I would not say that it changes anything in us physically.
It may. It may not. That depends on our samskaras and what Babuji wants for us. But it makes an absolutely fundamental change
in our existence because, for the first time, we have stopped
thinking of ourselves. And if this change is not brought about in
your life as an abhyasi, any benefits you may get from meditation
and cleaning, they are only temporary.   (p.129)

We must be grateful to the Master for providing to us, today,
such a simple way, you see, where without much effort, much
meditation, much cleaning, I mean, much of anything, we are
able to achieve that glorious goal. And I hope all of you will at
least put in the minimum effort and help Him to help you. (p.190)

So from the simple understanding, you see, that to know
honey, I must taste honey, I must be with honey, and to have the
real taste I must be healthy, I came to the greater understanding,
that for a yogic relationship with the Maker, you see, with the
Creator, we have to be in the presence of that which we want to
learn or understand. And we must be clean, absolutely clean, to
receive that. Otherwise it is like looking at something with coloured glasses on, and we can only see what this glass shows us,
not reality which is beyond.

Therefore, in the system of yoga that my Master taught us,
called Sahaj Marg, the cleaning of the heart of all its tendencies is
a very important aspect of our daily practice. And it is the heart
which gives the answers. And we have that small thing which is
called the conscience, you see, the voice of the conscience,
which, by being ignored life after life, hardly exists. In fact, I
think it exists like one of these small tiny flames, pilot flame, you
find in a big water heater. But the major thing is not burning. So
my Master said, "Go to the heart, clean the heart, purify the heart.
And simultaneously go nearer and nearer the presence of that

which you want to understand, which you want to know, which you want to become. And without that nothing is possible."

(p.201-202)

So you see, absolute knowledge always evades us because, in this world of conditioned existence, the reality is hidden. Not because somebody is hiding reality with a screen, but because we have learned to condition ourselves and look at the world through our emotions, through our perceptions. Therefore again I repeat the need for purification of the system, very much like you clean the lens of a camera before you take a picture.

...True knowledge, true understanding, comes by refining ourselves by purificatory processes, nothing wonderful, nothing extraordinary. As simple, I repeat, as cleaning the lens of a camera, or the glass of the lens.

Therefore, in my Master's system, we have this important practice of the cleaning process. And in case we feel guilty about being dirty or unclean, let me tell you my Master said, "There is no need to feel guilty, because again there is nothing which can be called dirt. But when something is there which should not be there, it interferes with our progress and therefore we remove it." Soil and mud and dust on the farms and the fields are essential, otherwise we would not have our rice and wheat that we eat. But when they are on electrical equipment, electronic equipment, glass lenses, they interfere with our interpretation of what we see, and therefore we have to remove them.

I have found, even in my experience, that when we talk of cleaning, people rebel. They say, "Oh, I am not dirty." Now it is not a question of being dirty or clean in the conventional sense. It is the need to remove something which is interfering in my communication, with that which I have to communicate with. I think this is the greatest blessing that my Master conferred on me and other disciples of his, that he made it possible for us to indulge, or involve ourselves, in this cleaning process without feeling dirty.

..And therefore the Veda uses the very great and very significant example, a symbol, that knowing and understanding are like removing the dust from the surface of a mirror. So in that sense it is wrong to say that we are acquiring knowledge. We are only removing the lack of knowledge that we have from ourselves, by cleaning away the impediments to that right understanding, by referring knowing and understanding back to that in us which is the true source of knowledge and understanding — the heart! And therefore the system of Sahaj Marg raja yoga works on the heart of the human being. In this system we meditate on the heart. It is the heart that is purified, and in that sense my Master used to say that, "We have to be humanized first."   (p.208-211)

Spirituality is not a few sittings, is not a cleaning session, is not even a donation to the mission, however big it may be. It is a total submission and a submergence into his will.   (p.242)

In His Footsteps, Volume I
Shri P. Rajagopalachari

Next, we have a process of cleaning, of throwing off of our samskaras. Good and evil, happiness and sorrow, these must come to every one of us, because they are the result of the samskaras of our past actions. So we follow this cleaning process to throw off these samskaras. It is a process of self-purification.
     (p.42)

Dr. KCV: The abhyasi also has to do his work. The cleaning process must be done in the evening. It is very important. People may say it is just imagination — to think that waves of bliss are passing through you and that dirt and disease etc. are going out as smoke from the back! But it has been proved that this really does take place. When you mentally think of this cleaning going on, the force of such a sincere thought sets certain centres at work so that samskaras are dropped off.

Some people have posed the philosophic problem that when a clay brick is fired, does it become a brick instantaneously or by stages. In other words, is the transformation of a man's body instantaneous or does it take place in stages? I think it is all a matter of cleansing. It can happen at once, here and now. It may take all eternity! It depends on you.

CAR: Our Shastras prescribe the purificatory rite of Bhuta Suddhi. In principle this is the same.

Dr. KCV: In principle, yes. But what is the result? You know almost all religions talk somewhere or other of such purification. The Jains had it, this principle of cleansing. They called it *Nirjara* and *Samvara*. The *Nirjara* — not getting old or not being allowed to grow old; the *Samvara*, which should really be *Samyogvara* — meaning excellence. But unfortunately the Jains themselves don't know what these things mean today."

(To P.R.) Have you read the old issues of our *Sahaj Marg*? There (Year 7, Nos. 3 and 4) I have written a series of articles on the efficacy of Raja Yoga where I have treated of this particular subject. You know how Master has indicated points A and B, both of which fall within the region of the physical heart. Two fingers width to the right of the left nipple, and three finger widths below that, lies point A. Point B lies two finger widths below A. These two points have to be cleaned. As I have already told you, Master, or the preceptors, clean by Pranahuti, and it can also be done by one self. In fact has to be done, by the power of one's own thought. The process involves the prevention of extraneous impulses entering into the heart, thus upsetting its equilibrium; and also a throwing out of impulses which are already within, and which tend to settle as karmic residue or dust particles. These have to be cleaned out from there, naturally."

These are the two processes the Jains used to call *Nirjara* and *Samvara*. The entry of impulses into the heart, settling of particles, makes for old age. The sediment of such particles is familiar to students of philosophy as *pudgala*. The prevention of impulse-entry is therefore, in terms of ancient Jain terminology, *Nirjara*; while cleaning out the *pudgala* is *Samvara*.

In our system, the two processes are given a physical basis in the heart, at points A and B. We, in our practice, are advised to close point A to outside forces; simultaneously we must feel or imagine the divine forces working at Point B, and all the gross residue being thrown out at the back as smoke or vapour. (p.66-68)

In His Footsteps, Volume II
Shri P. Rajagopalachari

Master gave Sulochana a special sitting. As soon as I came home from the office Master told me, "I have examined my daughter-in-law again — now she is cleaned. Brother, I was a bit worried that it may not be any disease of the heart and that she may not have a heart attack. But there is no such thing. It was only heaviness, and that has now been cleared away."   (p.10)

We were all reluctant to have this excursion because on Tuesday last Master went out on a short tour of London and came back in almost a collapsed condition. On that occasion he could hardly climb up the stairs to his bedroom, and went to bed at once. Later on he told me that the atmosphere of London had been so heavy he had almost suffocated. When repeating this to Vera she asked him, "But Master, why did you not clean it?" Master said, "I cleaned it just enough so that I could live in it."

Vera: Master, is the London atmosphere as bad as that over Paris? We have always been told that there is so much that is bad in Paris, and so we feel that the atmosphere there must be very bad indeed.

Master: No. In Paris it was quite good, I had no trouble there. I find that the atmosphere over London is the worst of all I have seen.

Vera: Oh Master! Could you clean this, if it is so bad? It would be wonderful if you could.

Master: Yes. I told you I have already cleaned it a little — maybe five percent — but more I will not do. If people want then they must pray for that. (p.90-91)

In His Footsteps, Volume III
Shri P. Rajagopalachari

I felt tears coming into my eyes. I recalled without any volition on my part, or even the merest wish to do so, all the wonderful qualities of my beloved Master. The thought arose spontaneously and automatically in my mind, and I seem to recall, as if in recollection, Master's Divine Love for his abhyasis, his unfailing courtesy and gentlemanly behaviour even with the smallest of us, his permanent cheerfulness, his humour, etc. The thought came to my mind that perhaps this was an aspect of cleaning too. Perhaps the impressions created in my mind by these qualities of the Master — noble though they are — have also to be erased by cleaning! This was the next thought, the reason being that otherwise the love for the Master, which may be there, would be a love conditioned by the existence of these very qualities in the Master. A love dependent on these five qualities for its existence would be no true love. A further thought then surfaced: We human beings are all conditioned in our loves mainly because of the presence of such qualities in those whom we love. Take away those qualities, and the love too fades away. But true love must exist without the beloved having necessarily to possess any such qualities whatsoever. Then alone could the love be called 'true love'. This thought then expanded into its next thought: our Master loves us in precisely this way. Nay! Even where he would be justified in not loving us, such as when an abhyasi has repulsive or hateful qualities, even then Master is able to love the abhyasi. I then had a glimmering of an idea, a sort of timid realisation, of what Divine or Universal Love really is. Such a love pervades everything in the universe because such a love does not need any qualities, or characteristics, to love, and it therefore exists independently of all qualities in the beloved — good, bad, indifferent! All these thoughts came into my mind during this brief sitting, and revealed to me the nature of the cleaning process, how deeply it has to probe, and how comprehensive it has to be in its application and functioning.   (p.6-7)

We then went to bed. After I had gone to bed, Master suddenly asked me to sit in meditation and gave me a twenty minute sitting. About halfway through the sitting I had a vision in which I saw that I was dead, and my corpse was lying on the ground. When I told this to Master after the sitting, he smiled and said that it was an indication of the deepening of *layavastha*. I asked him how deep my *layavastha* was. He laughed and said that it was not possible to fix degrees or percentages of *layavastha*. He then added that he had cleaned some of the chakras in the system. We went to sleep after this at around 11:00 P.M.   (p.22)

I told Master about this attitude of Umesh with great reluctance when I was at Shahjahanpur for Basant in February. Master said, "I don't know what has happened to my sons. Prakash has become very egotistic." My problem is, what do I do when Master comes to Madras on 2 May 78 after his Bangalore visit? He is to stay here for a period of five days. He will naturally stay with Umesh. How can I go to meet Master if Umesh continues to behave like this? The irony is that to the best of my knowledge I have given no cause for anger or annoyance. In fact we have met hardly at all. The whole affair is very puzzling to me, and causing me much sorrow. At night, I prayed to Master for nearly half an hour to set things right, and then worked on Umesh and cleaned his heart. Let me see what the result is going to be. (p.135-136)

Later Master remarked to me, "Before one sits in meditation, or before one gives a sitting to others, one should do one's cleaning first. It is enough if this cleaning is done for a few minutes. This confers much benefit. How did you feel today? You are completely full!" (p.260)

Love and Death
Shri P. Rajagopalachari

So you see, this idea of the past having such a terrible hold on our future that it makes us impotent or it makes us keep going in circles. Let me do that which I am accustomed to do, it is safe, it is secure. It is a fallacy. Because if I am going to continue to do the very same things that I have done, in the understanding that it is safe — there is no safety in repetition. So you see, we have to forget the past and in Sahaj Marg we don't have to forget it but we can remove it altogether by cleaning, it is one of the great benefits. I think it is a revolutionary concept in spirituality. I have often said that cleaning, in my mind, is more important than transmission. Because if we transmit without cleaning, we are only perpetuating the same condition in a stronger and stronger form. (p.14)

Who needs time? One who has not used this time profitably — he needs more and more time. "Give me three more days!" Every man who is dying, it is said, prays, "Lord, give me a few more hours or few more days in which I can change the past, so that I can change my future!" It is too late! Because when we have left the past unchanged for long, it is like sediment in a river which becomes harder and harder and becomes rock. Now you have to blast it. Therefore the daily cleaning. Clean it while it is still possible for you to clean. If you cannot clean it today, tomorrow it will be harder! Day after tomorrow it will be even more hard. Why? Because now there are three layers of grossness. The lowest very hard, little less hard, soft. You will only be able to clean the top, the bottom keeps on hardening. So what is worth doing must be done now, what is not worth doing should never be done.

(p.25-26)

So you see, deserving-ness and undeserving-ness are qualities we as abhyasis have to develop in ourselves. It is an aspect of humility, an aspect of craving that, "I, my Lord, who am looking for you to inhabit me, I feel myself worthless of your presence. I feel this abode of yours which is in me, is unclean. It is unfit to receive you." In that sense I am undeserving.

Sahaj Marg says, clean yourself. It is very simple. After all, this was a horse stable and see today how beautiful it is. So you see, if I want, or if anyone wants, to become divinised, it means an absolute injunction upon that person.   (p.37)

So, if every mother's child is perfect, how can there be imperfect people? So when you think you are imperfect, you are already starting with a criticism of your creator. "I am imperfect." 'I' am never imperfect. My actions are imperfect, my thoughts are imperfect, my giving is imperfect, my taking is imperfect. I am imperfect in my thoughts and actions. 'I' am not imperfect. 'I'

am never imperfect because 'I' my Master created, my God created. He never created imperfect things.

Therefore when we clean we are removing these imperfections, and here in Sahaj Marg the perfection also, because the law says, "You cannot get rid of the duality of existence. You cannot remove imperfection and leave perfection behind." You take both or you leave both. Therefore when we take away all that is in you which is not created by Him, then remains that which He created, which is the Perfect. So here there is no good, there is no bad, there is only the idea of perfection.   (p.56)

Everything natural is not permanent. There is a flower today, it is not there tomorrow. There are the flowers today, tomorrow they are gone. But this must be here as a permanent presence. That presence will attract people from everywhere, make them share in this joy that has been created here, the spiritual joy. Sharing that presence, become something like that presence, progressively — this is our job.

"How to do it?" she asks. There is a nice old story about an emperor who was very fond of art. Perhaps I have said this before. And he wanted to have an art competition, and he invited artists from all over the world. And he told his chief minister, "Give each one a large hall, and ask them to adorn the walls, and at the end we will judge and give prizes." So, artists from all over the world came. Each one had a hall. They were all painting, you know, furiously. Big brushes, small brushes, oils, water colours, crayons, everything. The Chinese group came. They partitioned the wall, because somebody was painting there. They said, "We only want some grinding materials." Everybody was surprised, "What will they do with it?" They said, "On the final day when the King judges, then only will we open our studio, not before that." And here next to them was the greatest artistry, beautiful you know, it was as if nature was open to reveal them — trees and birds and all colours, you know, riot of colours! Art! On the final day the King came, and he was going from hall to hall. Each one was better than the previous one. The final one, it was so fantastically beautiful, the King almost swooned. And he was about to award the prize when the minister said, "Majesty, there is one more you have to judge — the Chinese." He said, "Yes, let me, then." The Chinese opened the curtain, and on this side he saw the most beautiful painting that he had ever seen and he really swooned. When he woke up out of the swoon, he said, "Award the prize to them! How did you manage this?" They said, "Majesty, we did nothing. We polished the wall so beautifully, that it is reflecting this painting." So polish your wall so beautifully that it reflects the divine presence. You have nothing else to do. We are not going to create.

It's not like a baby, you know, you have to make. "Chari, how do you make a baby?" Nobody has asked me yet, even teenagers. They know all about it. But this is so easy! All that you do is to clean it, make it a mirror, voilà! Everything is there, you see. So there is no doing, there is only cleaning, cleaning. You are always cleaning your silverware service and your glassware and your beautiful stainless steel, which is so attractive and so very expensive. Do it inside and he that is outside, you will find is actually inside. So you see, you all have a very pleasurable duty and an opportunity for your own development, and to help the rest of the world to participate in this development. I wish you all joy with it.   (p.99-101)

So we are here to learn how to take out the best from every aspect of life. Not to look at the worst, but to look at the best. Then we shall have a positive approach, a properly oriented approach in which we can really help others.

Because if you are only going to see the sickness, the dirtiness, the ugliness, we are only fit to be sweepers. One who sees dirt everywhere, ugliness everywhere, filth everywhere, I would give him a broom and say, "Sweep that dirt. Clean it, that's all you are fit for, because you don't see anything else." It is said of the pig, which is the only animal that cannot look up, "It's always looking down." *Cochon*, and it's a fact. (p.116)

So you see, some of these few things I thought, I have been wanting to speak for the last few days. I am getting more and more reluctant to speak, but at the same time this was as if, you know, I had to throw it out. Maybe a personal cleaning was required for me, that I get rid of so many things from me, because I don't need these concepts anymore. For a person who has faith, knowledge is unnecessary. (p.126-127)

Revealing the Personality
Shri P. Rajagopalachari

So you see how stupid we are, to become bound to space and time, to be battered about by our sense of values and qualities, and to suffer from our own punishments and our own rewards, which we create because of feelings of pride for good actions so-called, and the feeling of so-called culpability for so-called wrong actions. Here, the ancient yoga psychology comes to our rescue, and says, "So long as you are bound to this body and the body con-sciousness, the suffering is inevitable. Separate yourself from this body. Even while you are in it, try to separate yourself from it. Try to become the observer of your actions, not the participator in your activity." And as you practise this more and more correctly, more and more, shall we say, systematically, you certainly become an observer, even of your own self. And constant remembrance, of course, is a big help.

So we have this wonderful idea, this liberating idea that 'I' do nothing, it is my body which is working according to the pushes and pulls of the samskaras. So, such an observer becomes capable of saying, "I am not responsible, because I don't act. I don't do anything. It is my samskaras, not me." So you see the importance of cleaning. Once the cleaning is going on and on, samskaras are gone, there is no more automatic reaction to situations, and we really become Masters in that sense that now we can do what we choose to do, and not because we are **bound** to do it. When you say, "I am bound to do something," it is a very real statement of bondage, that such a person has no choice.　　　　(p.41-42)

So don't think of rebirth as a punishment. God does not punish. The devil has no power to punish. In spirituality, there is no devil except the devil in each one of us. So if there is a devil, it is right there in you. Spirituality says, push the blighter out. Send him out, you know, he doesn't have any space in your heart. Why do you keep him there? So we have this immensely beneficial, effective system of cleaning in Sahaj Marg. All our samskaras make us a devil. When you remove the samskaras, there is that which is eternally present, a glorious light, the divine presence. So we don't have to bring God from somewhere and put Him into you. It is like cleaning out the rubbish to put in the new furniture. And that rubbish, all of it put together, is the devilish part, the dark part, the, shall we say, the baser part of each one of us.

So the cleaning is very important in Sahaj Marg. I personally believe that without cleaning you will not get anywhere. People are afraid of cleaning for several reasons. During cleaning, you may have experiences of the past, your actions, your thoughts, which created those impressions. Some may be good. Some may be awful. When you have a view that you are on, say, the Himalayas, trekking up there and planting a flag on Mount Everest, you are very proud. Suppose you have the same view of having gone almost to Mount Everest, but you fell down and crashed three thousand metres to your death, you come out screaming and you say, "No, no, this is not what I came to Sahaj Marg for." And getting nightmares — it is not a nightmare. Every dream, every nightmare, is something in you which is being released. You know, if a man is afraid of going to the toilet because he doesn't like what is coming out of him — he doesn't like its smell, he doesn't like its feel — and he tries not to go to the toilet, he will die. Isn't it?

So, people who are afraid of their samskara and keep it in their hearts, hidden, ashamed of it, guilty about it, afraid that when it comes out it may recreate some scene in which it was originally created — they are like people who will not go to the toilet: they will die. And that's what happens to people who don't clean themselves spiritually. They have no spiritual future. Therefore, in a very real spiritual sense, they die to come back.

So in spirituality we say, death is only there when we have not decided to go on beyond death but to come back because of our fears, because of our attachments. So please understand very carefully that if you have been able to clean yourself of all your samskaras and, through meditation, create a greater and greater illumination in yourself through the divine presence that is eternally there, there is no death for us. We leave the body behind, like you get out of the taxi, you get out of the train, you get out of the airplane, and go home. So fear has to go.   (p.50-51)

"What you have done in the past, you cannot change." Absolutely. It is finished. But, does it mean I am condemned? No. Why? Because I have a right to change my life in such a way that the past has no effect upon me — through cleaning, through meditation. Cleaning gets rid of the past, meditation creates the future, remembrance now prevents me from indulging myself in my fancies. In His remembrance, what I do is always right. So you see, the three instruments of Sahaj Marg — cleaning, meditation, constant remembrance — in my mind, they are infallible, unbeatable, totally effective instruments.   (p.54)

Spirituality says, "Nonsense. Simple things: He whom you worship, whom you seek, whom you have sought through eternity outside, seek him here. He is right there. How to seek him? Close your eyes. Get in touch with him through meditation." "But I have lost contact." "Go to someone who would restore that contact for you." "Where can I find him?" "Pray. He will come to you." "How do I know he is the right man?" "Sit and see. Meditate and see." "But he has been there, then why am I so miserable?" "Because of your samskaras." "Now, what shall I do about it?" "Clean yourself." "Is it possible?" "Yes." "By whom?" "You, yourself." "Will it be effective?" "Yes, if you lead your life properly. Perhaps not, if you choose not to. Not at all, if you deliberately go against your conscience and do things which you should not."   (p.57)

Nature needs all these things. We are only a part of that — maybe an important part, maybe a part destined to play a role in a future that we have to create for all of life. When you change something in a painting, you don't only change that something, you change the whole thing. The whole painting changes. So, if I am changing myself, the whole universe must change. And that is what philosophy says, that is what religions have preached: change yourself and the universe changes. But if you try to change that, you cannot make a duck into a peacock. Isn't it? So the secret of universal change is to change yourself.

Now, to change myself, again we come to this problem of attitudes, desires, likes and dislikes, all because of samskara. So Sahaj Marg says, "Clean it out." But people want to clean out selectively. "Oh, yes, all this can go, Chari, but this I don't want to leave." Yes, but it's either all or nothing! Isn't it? All or nothing is the formula for success, or failure, in spirituality. I want to remind you that there is no success or failure attached to the Master. He is doing his work. Success or failure is yours.   (p.67)

Imagine how coal was manufactured on earth by nature in the carboniferous age of this world, over an enormous period of time. The forests were compressed — enormous pressure, which a tree cannot normally bear. Coal is the result. In another way, under heat and pressure, it becomes a diamond. Nothing comes without heat and pressure. They are forces of nature which mould us in the right way. All your beautiful glass — melted in furnace, moulded in moulds, or blown, etc.

So you see, we need pressure under which to develop, and our samskaras are such pressures. They are for our benefit. If we think of our samskaras as our enemies, they become our enemies. If we think of them as our friends, they help us to mould ourselves, and to become what the Master wants. Now of course, you may ask why we are cleaning the samskaras? Samskaras work naturally over a long period of time in moulding you. And then, only if you are wise and you don't oppose their working. We don't have that wisdom, because everything that happens to us, we are opposing. Uncomfortable life — we want to make it comfortable. Painful life — we want to make it painless. We want to change our wife!

So you see, we are opposing samskara. Samskaras have no chance to mould us in the right way, and instead of working off these samskaras, we allow them to remain in the samskara bank, and by our willful action in the opposing direction, we are adding more to the samskara. Imagine what would happen to such a soul. Imagine what is going to happen to all the people of this world who are trying to better their life, as they say. Life is to be lived, not bettered. If we live life according to the way in which we are born and destined to live it here, that life will automatically improve in its stature. Not in material comforts, perhaps, though it is not ruled out. You will not become intelligent, but it is not necessary, because the soul in its wisdom before this birth, has allowed its samskaric burden to bring a particular life here for us. It is neither wise nor unwise. It is neither logical nor illogical. It is what is exactly necessary. That being so, if we obey that plan, our life will naturally improve.

Then, why do we clean samskaras? I come to that point again. Because, this process, like the manufacture of coal by nature, takes millions of years for the normal person. Though again, for a wise person, one life is enough. Because if in my life I have the samskara of suffering, and if I am living just a natural life, I may not be able to finish the samskara in one life. But if I welcome some sufferings, more and more and more, the samskara bank is being rapidly exhausted, and I can achieve my spiritual evolution in one life.   (p.126-127)

Now, number two: samskaras affect absolutely the physical existence. It would be foolishness to expect our physical life to change by spiritual practise. We cannot change our sex — absolutely fixed. We cannot change the figure — absolutely fixed. Then what are we going to change? So, the physical existence with which I have come, will follow me till I am dead.

Then what is the idea of cleaning? You know, if you buy a crystal glass and clean it, it does not change its form, but it becomes a fit receptacle for something you can put into it now. So, by cleaning that which was unfit, it becomes fit to receive the grace of the Almighty. This is the correct idea of cleaning. It does not mean a poor man will become rich, or an ugly girl beautiful, or a weak man become a strong man, though I must say, there will be normalisation of all functions.

So, cleaning must be understood very critically. Cleaning does not affect the physical existence, in the sense that my body cannot be changed, the colour of my hair cannot change, the colour of my eyes cannot change, etc. But the **quality** of my life will change.   (p.151)

The centre is not a place. It is not a thing. It is not a location in space or time. So, how to search for it? How to look for it? How to seek it? When? How? Why? All this is simple when we sit in meditation.

Now, what opposes this simple process? Ideally, there should be only meditation and nothing else. But we need, unfortunately, other processes like cleaning and constant remembrance. Why? Again, to make it possible that meditation succeeds, eventually, in our plunging into ourselves, and finding out that my Self is much more immense than any cosmic universe outside, or super-cosmic universe outside me. The cleaning removes what I have created for myself as samskaras, which have been pushing me and pulling me here and there, and makes me now do things by myself. Constant remembrance is to keep the mind employed so that it doesn't wander.

So you see, there is an immense body of sense behind what we are doing in this simple act of meditation and cleaning and re-membrance. Let us not complicate it with the mental acrobatics of the so-called intelligent and refined thinking mind of the West, which is a disease.   (p.188)

We are more worried today about external pollution, about the ozone layer, about the forests in Europe dying because of pollu-tion, about the rivers not being fit even for fish to live in. What about this universe **within**, which we have polluted over millen-nia of existence from the moment we were first created, and thrown out of our original home by our ego? Have we cleaned it up? Have we ever thought that if we cleaned this up, it will auto-matically become clean? Is it not this inner greed, lust, that is polluting the outer universe of mine? Is the outer universe any-thing other than the reflection of my inner universe? Therefore, is not the possibility of cleaning the external universe only latent in my cleaning up my inner universe? Otherwise, I am only cutting the grass and, you know, gilding the lily, as they say.

If this wisdom dawns, then who will **not** come to meditate? Who will **not** subject himself or herself to the cleaning process? Now, you may ask a question, "But Chari, you are talking about not-doing. But are you not **doing** cleaning?" Yes. But am I doing it? Babuji Maharaj said, "The merest suggestion, supposition of light." It is what we call a *sankalpa*. The difference between thinking and *sankalpa* is about just thinking and putting your will behind that thought. "I **will** do it," means I have willed myself to do it. "I will do it," does not mean that "I shall do it," or "I must do it." It does not mean anything of that sort. It means I have willed myself to do it, and it shall happen.   (p.221)

So you see, to suppose without supposing, to imagine where imagination is not possible, because all imagination is based on fact. To know that several lives have to be taken sometimes to work out a dominant trait or a dominant relationship — marrying the same person again and again and again, the same tragic sequence. A very small, beautiful book shows this again and again, *The Strange Life of Ivan Osokin.* One of the disciples of Gurdjieff wrote it. It is called 'eternal recurrence' in another language. Cyclical, going round and round until something gives you a push in a tangential direction, and you go into another sphere. That is the function of the spiritual life, and since it cannot be done from inside, it has to be done from outside. Therefore the Master! Therefore spirituality. Therefore meditation, cleaning, constant remembrance, nine o'clock prayer, etc.

...So, cleaning is not enough. All right, somebody cleans. But along comes an Indian, opens his envelope, throws it on the pavement, reads the news and goes. Somebody has to clean it again. We are doing it with our insides all the time. Somebody is cleaning, and we are creating. Again this idea, that when we try to create, we are only creating grossness — inside and outside. Which engineer is there who has created a miracle in my heart — a bridge between me and my beloved in my heart, one of these spidery, beautiful things on Lake Geneva which looks hardly capable of sustaining the load of one car. Where is that engineer?

(p.261-262)

Then what should we do? We have to come into the yogic path, of course. Do the cleaning, because as we remove the samskaras our personality changes. I don't mean that from inefficient we will become efficient, or that a bad scientist will become a good scientist, or that a bad gambler will become a good gambler. Not at all. We will approach more and more what Babuji calls human perfection.

(p.267)

Heart of the Lion
Shri P. Rajagopalachari

So I would like to tell you that these material pitfalls into which everybody can slip anytime, but for the help of God — because they are in your samskaras, they are pushing you inevitably, inexorably towards that particular pit — only the Master can save you by removing that samskara. But we don't go to him. We try to build fences, and a man comes and jumps over the fence. We build a wall, another climbs over the wall and jumps, just to see what is on the other side of the wall. Something which is so carefully protected must have something wonderful inside. Isn't it?

So forget these sensory pitfalls, worldly pitfalls. These are everybody's cup of poison, cup of misfortune. There is relief, but only from and through the Master. He can help us by cleaning off all our tendencies, our samskaras, so that these pitfalls are as if they have been filled up with sand, and no more in my path. But the big pitfalls — the pitfall of misunderstanding, the pitfall of wrong expectations — these are the **real** pitfalls which block our path, which make progress impossible. Not because **he** is help-less, but because **we** are helpless.

So, please try to understand spirituality properly. What is a Master? Why is he **my** Master? It is not because I am his slave. The Western people rebel at this idea, you see, that because he is my Master, I must be his slave. "I don't want to be anybody's slave. I am a great man myself. I am the chairman of, I don't know, the Federal Bank of Johannesburg. Or I own De Beers, so why do I need a Master?" You need a Master precisely because there are things in you — you may be the best diamond miner yourself, but he can mine something from inside you — the dirti-est things which are lying hidden, which are not accessible to anybody, not even to yourself, after removing which you are richer than if you have all the diamonds of this world with you. Here, it is by un-becoming, un-doing.

In Sahaj Marg the world is not to become something. We un-become until we are what we were. It is like a person undressing to expose his naked self which is as he was born with. To do this, it is like cleaning the sewers. You have a special class of people who come to clean your sewers, who are willing to go down into that muck, into that stink, and clean it for you. That is why Babuji said, "I am really in the sewers and gutters of humanity." Imagine what a person must be capable of — what suffering, what forti-tude, what courage, what bravery, that he goes into this hellhole of existence and comes out clean — not only clean himself, but cleaning you also in the process. Are we or are we not going to accept such a person's service? If we are, do we know what serv-ice he is really doing for us? If we appreciate that, is there a price that we can pay which can ever be too much for the service he is rendering? Can it [be] evaluated in terms of rands?   (p.110-112)

What is Sahaj Marg A Preceptor's Guide, Volume I
Shri P. Rajagopalachari

Hell is created by our own wrong thoughts, wrong actions, grossness. So if there is a hell, and Babuji has said there **is**, it must be, it is a creation of our grossness. So when people come to me and say, "Oh, I am suffering the tortures of hell." Of course, we cannot be unkind and say, "Yes, suffer it! Because you have created it." (laughter) We cannot. As preceptors it is our duty to be generous, to be kind, to be loving, which our Master is always; do the cleaning, give a little transmission and, if necessary, speak a few words of love and send him away with confidence and, more necessary, hope. (p.31)

You see, it's like a lamp, the glass chimney of which has been coated with soot from inside. The lamp is burning but there is no light coming out. So this is the thing of which Babuji used to say, "Even criminals have this light within them." We don't see it because they have enshrouded it within that enormous solidity of the grossness that they have accumulated. When you clean it away you find the light is still within them too.

Therefore in Sahaj Marg we are taught, I mean, Babuji insists, that while we can hate what a man does or a woman does, don't hate the person himself or herself because the person is always divine. For the nonce there is something wrong with it, because it is covered over with slime, with mud. Clean it away and it is as pure as you are. (p.34)

I must allow my source to flow out of me, you see. Which means, when such a man speaks it is divine, when he says something it is divine, when he talks it is divine, when he walks it is divine — everything that he does. Because, it is not he who is doing it, it is the inner spring in him which is welling out through him. And this is possible only by cleaning away the samskaras, and transmitting to him the essence of the Master which we [the preceptors] have all been permitted to do.   (p.36)

Now cleaning. It's a very obvious thing we all know. As I have said so many times, if I have stored gasoline in a bottle and I wish to buy milk in it, I have to clean it first. So when we are trying to put something into us which is of the highest order of existence, the divine essence of the Master by way of his transmission, we have to make ourselves fit to receive it. That is the cleaning process.   (p.56)

So the cleaning for ourselves is very important because we depend on it for our personal evolution, in the sense that unless our heart is clean the Master is certainly not going to come and occupy it. And unless it is absolutely clean, he is not going to stay in it. So it is the need of the hour, the need of eternity, to purify the heart to such an extent and to keep it so pure that He will not leave that place even if you want to push him out.   (p.59)

Now when we talk of a mission, this instinctive revulsion, revolt against the word 'mission', you should kindly remove from your minds, it can be done by cleaning — one technique.   (p.73)

So please remember the importance of cleaning, the importance of yatra. Without cleaning there is no yatra. It is not possible. Therefore the importance of the preceptor. People often ask, "Why preceptors? Cannot Babuji do it himself?" Of course he can. But to assist him in his work and to speed his work on the abhyasis, to make it possible for them to achieve their goal quicker, he uses preceptors to do what **we** might think of as the dirty work — cleaning! In a sense, it is dirty work. In a sense, it is very noble, you see, when you can prepare a person for liberation, it is by no means dirty. So this is the importance of the yatra, and it must be correctly understood, because without a correct understanding and appreciation of the yatra you are not going to understand the implications and the importance of cleaning, whether for yourself or for those who come to you. **Without cleaning, there is no yatra!** Write it in red ink! (p.86)

So this heart region, coming back to that mess you see, which is the most difficult place to clean, Babuji once told me that sometimes he felt as if he was under the sewer systems of a big metropolis — nowhere to go, dark everywhere, stinking. You are afraid to fall because if you fall into that mire you will never rise again. Awful demons, imagination and reality around you. Rats, sewer rats you know, are supposed to be the biggest. And Babuji's face took on such an expression, you would have pitied him if you had seen it. And there was an occasion when he prayed to Lalaji, "Why have you put me in this gutter?" And Lalaji said, "Which gutter? That is in a human being, and you are there to clean it. Clean it!" And the generosity of the Master you know — Babuji told me once that he was in a city called Benares in the centre of India, a holy city, the holiest of holy cities in India. But it has its own red-light district. Inadvertently Babuji wandered into it. He didn't know where he was going. And as he was walking through those streets, Lalaji's voice came from above, "My friend, what are you doing here?" Babuji was shaken. I mean, Babuji was really shaken, you see. He said, "Saheb," — Saheb means Master — "I don't know where I am, I don't know what I am doing." Lalaji said, "Well, this is not the place where you should be, but since you have come, clean it." You see, there was no choice! A broom, wherever it is, has to do the cleaning, you see. If it is in the bedroom it cleans the bedroom. If it is in the toilet it cleans the toilet. If it is in the throne room it cleans the throne room too. It has no choice, you see, it can only clean. Therefore Babuji said, "I am the vacuum cleaner. I clean anything that has to be cleaned." In cleaning we cannot distinguish between good dirt and bad dirt, superior dirt and inferior dirt. You know, it's like a barber shop in South Africa where they will remove the white man's hair from the floor but not the black man's perhaps. Hair is hair, you see.   (p.99-100)

So please don't underrate this cleaning. It is of the utmost significance, it is of utmost importance, even to the Master himself. Because until **you** clean, **he** cannot do anything about it. And once he had to write a letter to a centre in India from where I think eight or ten abhyasis had gone to be with Babuji for three days. Babuji wrote back to the head of that centre, "I am happy that you sent these people to me. I like to see my abhyasis when they come. And I like to serve them in my own way — but I am sorry that you sent them in such a sordid condition, that all the three days they were here I could spend only in cleaning. I could not advance them further. I regret to say that you have failed in your duty towards me and the Mission. Had you but done the cleaning necessary, they would have benefited much by coming to me. Now that benefit has been denied." It was a very stern letter from the Master, you see, very rare! Babuji rarely wrote such letters. So you can imagine what anguish he must have suffered that those abhyasis were there, and he was not able to do anything, but could do only the cleaning!   (p.100-101)

So I cannot sufficiently emphasize the importance of cleaning for ourselves, for the abhyasis who come to us. It is of the utmost importance, there is nothing more important than that in Sahaj Marg. Transmission comes only after cleaning. You know the dictum that, "If you transmit to a thief, you'll only make him a better thief. If you continue to transmit you'll make him a perfect thief." Transmission without cleaning can actually damage a person. So transmission is always done only after sufficient cleaning has been done. That is why we give these introductory three sittings which are devoted solely to cleaning. No trans-mission at all. (p.102)

And it is important that you avoid making impressions. You hear so many things, you see so many things, immediately you react and you create an impression, you weep, you make a scene; it creates an even deeper impression in the person concerned, and then it may take months to clean that out. (p.153)

I find this tendency in the West, which is rather unthoughtful and unnecessary, that when an abhyasi starts weeping, immediately you go and hug him or her and say, "No, no, darling, cheri," whatever it is, you see — kiss them — "Please don't weep." They must weep, you see. Promote it if possible. Leave them alone if you can't. If you have not the courage to bear it, leave them alone. Let them weep, because in that lies their salutary progress. It is inner cleansing at the deepest. (p.187)

The subtler the grossness, the more difficult it is to remove. I have to finally give another talk on cleaning, maybe, because it's the most important thing in Sahaj Marg. If you read my first book, *India in the West,* you will find all the lectures I gave in Europe were devoted to cleaning — basically, you see. Babuji said, "Speak about cleaning, the importance of cleaning." It is most important. (p.213)

When you come back out of remembrance the tendency is there, because the grossness is there. Now, for a man who is clean, and in constant remembrance, nothing can happen. What do we do? Either we are slipping in and out of remembrance, which is no longer constant remembrance, and we are subjected to this world. When we are here, we are subjected to this, the law of gravitation, let us say. When we are here, we are pulled up. We are like a yo-yo, you know, moving up and down. And in the higher up people, they are fully clean, but they are not in remembrance. See the two have to go together. Absolutely. Clean system and constant remembrance. If the two are there, instant saint.

(p.217)

...I gave you that example, you know — cleaning can never cause harm, so it's for your good. And all the lightness that you feel during a sitting is not due to transmission at all, it's due to cleaning. Cleaning gives you lightness. Transmission, when you are light, gives you the feeling of going deep into the meditation.

(p.265)

A brick, when it falls from here (a large height) only kills. Isn't it? If it's on the floor, at the most, you may stub your toe on it. So elevation carries with it the potential for both. Therefore cleaning is more and more important. As Babuji said, "Don't give power without cleaning." That is why these three preparatory sittings, which can be, or which generally is, even more sometimes. Babuji said once he gave twenty-two sittings to a man before starting transmission.

(p.267)

Q: But if we came from the source, why is all this trouble and suffering to go back to the source?

PR: Read the literature. (laughter) It's all given there. You see, the simple example: we have in gaseous form water vapour — it's free; it is mobile; it can move anywhere; it cannot be contained; it can expand or contract at will. It falls as rain — it is already limited by its form; it can still be mobile, but not as it was. And when you condense it further it becomes ice — it is solid, immovable, heavy, everything, you see. The thing is the same. This is gross, that is subtle. So Babuji used to say, "The human being is gross, God is the subtlest." Therefore, as we drop our grossness by cleaning, by change of our ways of life, we become subtler and subtler and approach the divine state. So again you come to that point, which I was saying, there is no evolution as such. Only thing, you are giving up the grossness. (p.322)

A Preceptor's Guide, Volume II
Shri P. Rajagopalachari

So please don't look for grossness. Transmit, wait. It's like a radar you know, it is not looking for something. If there is something it reflects the information back. It doesn't say, "Oh, I don't find anything here." We are not supposed to find. When it is not there, good. It is a state of beatitude of which we should be very grateful to the Master. "Ah, I found an abhyasi in whom there is nothing today." "No, no, but there must be grossness because Master said there is a human being and he cannot exist without grossness, let me look for it." See, it becomes a very morbid turn of the mind. Like a physician examines a patient who comes to him and says, "Oh, there is no disease in you, but I'm sure there must be something otherwise you wouldn't have come to me. Let me go through you again." And takes his knives and scalpels and what-not and cuts him open to see where the disease is, and destroys him.

We are unable to find the grossness in ourselves, and this has been reported to me by many preceptors. They say when I do the cleaning I don't find anything in myself to clean, precisely for the same reason, that if it isn't there, why are you looking for it? Just do the cleaning you see. It's like a man who is washing himself in the shower. I know some people who do it, soap themselves and look at the soap suds to see how black it is. You know, they derive a satisfaction out of the cleaning process. I know a lady who once came out of the bathroom to show me the shampoo from her hair, you see how black it is. (laughter) I said, "It's not necessary for me to see it. I know it is there, that's why I told you to shampoo your hair." (laughter, he chuckles) So you see, this morbidity, this is again an inculcation of religion. "Repent for your sins." "Yes, but I am not conscious of sins, for which sins shall I repent?" "Aha! Since you are asking this question you must have committed many sins." You know, it is so cruel to the abhyasis. It is so cruel to the self.

I told you the story last year when I, when Babuji asked me, "Do you do the cleaning?" And I said no. He said "Why?" He put on a frown, he tried to look serious. He said, "Why?" I said, "I have never felt dirty. When I don't feel dirty, I don't feel the need to clean myself." I thought he would reprimand me and pull me down a few points for my arrogance. (laughter) But he patted me on the back and said, "Shabash, this is what I want. You see, why do people think of grossness all the time? That is my problem. Not yours." You see, a state of innocence does not mean that we are not dirty. It means that we are not conscious of our dirt. A child is dirty all the time. It is innocent, it is pure, the mother hugs it, the parents hug it, the grandparents hug it, kiss it with all its filth on its face — chocolate smears. We find it so adorable. Not because it is not unclean but because it is so pristinely innocent that it is not conscious of anything, you see. The real sin, to my mind, is the consciousness of sin.   (p.23-25)

Preceptors think that because they are giving sittings to others, they don't need to meditate themselves, they don't need to do the evening cleaning, under the pretext that they are too busy.

No individual can ever be too busy to avoid the personal sadhana at any time until a stage comes when the Master says it is no more necessary for you. There does come a stage when Babuji said, "Stop. For you, no more meditation. No more cleaning. You look after my work." Till then, this does not stop. Morning meditation, evening cleaning, night time prayer meditation are an eternal companion of the abhyasi and also of the preceptor who is in his own self an abhyasi. Please remember this.   (p.57-58)

Preceptors must take individual sittings from one another for purposes of cleaning. This also helps to avoid the development of egoism, that one preceptor is greater than the other.   (p.58)

And since it is not a physical conduit, it is something spiritual, therefore, the need for moral values, values of the soul as we call them. Therefore, we don't speak much of bodily cleanliness in Sahaj Marg, though Babuji does say, "When you start meditation, you must have enough attention to purity of the body and the mind." Normally in India they bathe before they meditate. But that is not a strict requirement so long as you are clean. A bath doesn't necessarily mean you are clean. Often it is possible to be quite dirty.

Psychologists will tell you that there is a different sort of uncleanliness. The classic symptom of a person always trying to wash his hands. Sitting everywhere he is doing this [motions as if washing his hands] all the time. As if there are soapsuds and he is washing his hands. It's a very classic symptom.

So it is that purity to which we refer. That which cannot be cleaned by water and soap. That has to be done by the cleaning of the interior, by the cleaning system that we have in this Mission, in this method, and to be able to do that effectively. I have given you the parallel at the last seminar in Courmettes. It is like a surgeon who scrubs his hands, puts on his gloves, puts on his sterile robes and whatever you have to put on, goes into a sterile theatre, operates under the conditions of strictest sterility — for the patient's good. That is an external sterilization, an external purification, to see that microbes, germs, what have you, don't go with you into the operation theatre and infect the patient whom you are trying to save.

Here the parallel is the inner cleanliness, the inner purity, so that we don't even by accident contaminate.   (p.72)

So transmission only augments the qualities that are already in you, in the abhyasi. Therefore the emphasis placed on the cleaning system, again and again, you see. I would suggest that the cleaning can never stop because, knowingly or unknowingly, as the cleaning proceeds we are creating more grossness in ourselves by thinking and doing things in a wrong way, in a negative way, in an undesirable way. So the cleaning is always proceeding. So it also means that as long as we are doing the cleaning and the transmission, there is also this possibility that as long as grossness is there the transmission will also have some negative effect to that extent.

...It is very necessary to understand that transmission by itself is of no use. If you put milk in a dirty vessel it is dirty, perhaps you cannot even drink it. If you continue to pour milk into it you are only making more and more milk useless. Instead of wasting a gallon, you are wasting two gallons, twenty gallons, two hundred gallons. The vessel must be cleaned first.   (p.78-79)

Because please be assured that by the power of the Master and his grace, anything can be corrected in an instant of time. All that it needs is the right thought, the will power to back it, and the subtlest suggestion that we should employ. It doesn't take time. That it takes time is our failure. That it doesn't take time for the Master is his greatness. All that we have to do is to try to bridge this gap between our failure and his greatness by creating in ourselves the love for the abhyasis that we want to transform them, wholeheartedly. Use the power that Babuji has given us for cleaning and for transmission, and employ the power of the mind in subtlest transmission and it shall be achieved.   (p.100)

So whether as an abhyasi or as a preceptor, sitting should be limited to a maximum of one hour, remembering that the minimum for an individual sitting is thirty minutes, at least twenty minutes to be devoted to only cleaning in the beginning.

If you feel that the work of cleaning is not over, you have the right to start it all over again mentally, and prolong the sitting.

(p.104)

The primary effort, or pursuit, under the system of Sahaj Marg training is therefore to look to the proper cleaning and regulation of the mind, at the very initial stage, so that the mind may be relieved of its grosser and inharmonious tendencies. My Master, Shri Babuji Maharaj, has bequeathed to us some processes for the cleaning of the abhyasis.

The preceptor should exercise his will to purge out all the undesirable elements from the abhyasis' hearts, and awaken in him the state of the Absolute which is dormant in him. By this process, the abhyasi will constantly get the necessary power required for his own spiritual upliftment, and his progress will be perfect and permanent.   (p.113)

But here what happens is that by the progressive cleaning, the latent powers which are lying dormant in the abhyasi they themselves come to his help from within him for his spiritual evolution. "This process is to be repeated when working with each point or chakra." This you know from reading *The Efficacy of Raja Yoga* there are these one, two, three, four points of the heart region. In practice you should, ideally speaking, clean each chakra. And when this is completely clean move on to the next, introduce a little, as Babuji calls it, light, and leave it at that.

(p.114-115)

— ❖ —

This really applies in a certain fashion to points below the heart. What you call the psychic centres — the spinal centres — the *muladhara*, the *swadhishthana*, the *manipura*. Really we don't work consciously on these centres. But, if you just have the awareness that, as you are doing the cleaning this must also be cleaned, you will find that the power radiates. After all it is radiating from a point in a fashion which you can define as circular. That is, it has a 360 degree radiation. Everything goes like that. This cleaning automatically affects the lower centre.

So that is why we don't touch the spinal points in our system.

(p.116)

— ❖ —

All the points of the traditional hatha yoga system are on the back and are located on the spinal column. So we don't touch those at all. But the mere idea that as I am cleaning the upper point the lower point gets cleaned, will itself be sufficient to do the cleaning. In the same way as this is cleaned, they will also get cleaned.

They should be taken up and cleaned while cleaning the heart.

...That is why I said we don't pay particular attention to the lower centres, but just have this thought that by the Master's grace the lower centres are being cleaned to the necessary extent while the upper centres are being cleaned by you. It is necessary to remember that too much cleaning of these centres really leads to awakening which is undesirable.   (p.117-118)

Now comes the cleaning for the abhyasis by themselves.

Cleaning is an extremely important part of the sadhana. My Master has recommended the following processes for use by abhyasis.

1) Daily use: (in their daily work): think that all the impurities are going out of your back in the form of smoke or vapour, and that (This is very important, I think this has been neglected in the past, even by me in talking to you, assuming that everybody knows, you see, but I suddenly found when I went through my notes I have not spoken about this to you in the past, nor have I written to anybody about it.) **Think all the impurities are going out of the back in the form of smoke or vapour And that in its place the sacred current of the Divine is entering into your heart from the Master's heart.**

I apologize for this omission in the past but perhaps this is why in many cases progress is retarded or stopped, because when something goes, something must take its place. So when we imagine the grossness, or the abhyasi imagines the grossness is going out of his heart from behind in the form of smoke or vapour, also imagine, he should imagine, or she should imagine, the abhyasi should imagine, that something is coming into its place from in front and that is the Master's grace from the Master's heart, to replace this grossness that has gone out. Please remember this. I repeat again, I apologize for my omission of this very important thing. I cannot understand how I did not mention it, but it is there.   (p.122)

3) For those who require drastic cleaning: Imagine (this is to be told to the abhyasi) **imagine that you are seated in the ocean of bliss — merged with it, merged inside it — and imagine that the waves of the ocean are passing through your entire body washing away all the grossness and impurities. Until you are able to perceive by yourself that your whole body has become crystal clear.**

Now, very often, you know, when this process was recommended by Babuji in the past, abhyasis would start it and stop it because they found no change. But that was because they didn't give it sufficient time. So whenever you use this it is only for drastic cleaning.

...So until you find in your reading that there is the need for this drastic cleaning because the abhyasi is not benefiting by the traditional cleaning which I spoke about at first, then only should it be recommended for them. This technique is not to be used by preceptors at all. I mean on the abhyasis. They may do it upon themselves when they feel the need to do so.

In all these processes, it is essential to apply the force of the will to throw out impurities and grossness out from the body and to end the cleaning with a feeling of confidence that the process has been efficiently carried out and that the system has been rid of its impurities.

You see, here comes the need for faith, confidence, and the application of will power. I think in Courmettes I had a discussion about meditation and cleaning, what is the basic difference. The basic difference is that in meditation your mind is brought to a state of passivity applied to a single object to promote or develop concentration, and there it rests. There is no question of will power during meditation. In cleaning there is no meditation, there is only the application of will power used to remove grossness, impurities, complexes, progressively, stage by stage, initially upon the whole heart when you don't have the capacity to read.   (p.124-125)

a) **Meditation on point 'A': The abhyasi should be instructed to fix his attention on the point A with the thought that all the men and women of the world are his brothers and sisters.**

This is a very positive meditation. We don't say, "Oh, such and such person is not my sister," because then she is something else. Especially for males, you see. You must have the positive thought, meditating on this point, all in this world are my brothers and sisters. And please don't make... (bringing the exclusion principle) and say, "except..." (laughter) (He laughs.) Yes, there is always a temptation to exclude something, you see, which for the moment is exciting. This is a total principle you know, that all are my brothers and sisters.

...So this is to be done with a mind which longs for correction. I know there are many people who are perverted, and who don't wish to change their pervert tendencies or their wrong deeds. Of such people you can expect nothing. And for them this technique will not work, because in the beginning they will refuse to employ it. They will say, "Why? I am happy as I am." This is for the sincere seeker, who, being aware of the tendencies of his mind, and who, deploring his own activities in the field of action, wishes to correct himself sincerely, honestly, towards correcting himself and divinising himself eventually. For such a person this technique is most effective.

Meditate on point A, with the thought that all the men and women of the world are his brothers and sisters. This meditation is to be done just before going to bed. (That is, instead of the cleaning process which you do. If you don't do it at the time it is stipulated, you normally do it at night, before the prayer meditation. This should be just before the prayer-meditation.) **for not more than ten minutes.**

Now people may ask "Why?" Because if this feeling becomes too deeply implanted in the heart, you know, instead of just producing a clean attitude towards humanity, it may produce what we deplore in Sahaj Marg, a running away from life all together.

You know, that all are brothers and sisters, how can I ever marry this girl? So you feel the need to give up life, give up marriage, become celibate, on the way to the jungle. It goes to the opposite extreme. Everything has an optimum time, an optimum effect, and for this meditation the optimum is ten minutes.

My Master has said that generally women do not require this meditation, as they are comparatively free from the restless tendencies. (He laughs;) (laughter) Since my Master has said it I won't question it. (laughter) **But if a sister abhyasi is a victim of such tendencies, then she may be advised to follow the process with a slight modification in the process. She should think that all divine gifts are available to her, and that all men and women of the world think they are brothers and sisters and that her thought is one with theirs.**

It's a rather convoluted way of achieving the same thing. She doesn't think that all men and women are her sisters. She thinks divine blessings are coming to her. That all the men and women of the world are meditating on this thought that they are all brothers and sisters, and that she is part of that thought. I think this is necessary in the case of women, because, as you know, they are the propagators of the race. Through women, of course, humanity breeds, you see, and if this tendency that all are brothers and sisters, and the tendency to celibacy and all these things go too far, and too many people, I mean, nowadays it may be desirable that the population is limited but in the future it might not be so desirable. So women are to practice the same technique on A point meditation with this slight change.[1]   (p.128-130)

Meditation on Point 'B': Fix the attention on the point B and imagine that all your impurities and grossnesses are going out from point B from the front of the body.

---

[1] You may get more information from your preceptor if necessary

In the general cleaning which you do, it is all from the back of the body as smoke or vapour. In this case it is to imagine that they are going out from the front especially from the point B.

Imagine that as this process is going on the glow of the Atman, the soul begins to appear from behind.

It is like cleaning a dirty light and as the cleaning goes on, the light is coming out more and more bright. So here also as this cleaning on point B goes on you have to imagine that the dirt and the filth all accumulated there is coming out. And as this cleaning is proceeding a glow begins to appear from behind which is the light of the *Atman*, you see, the soul. **This process is to be done in the morning, before beginning morning meditation but never more than for ten minutes.**

So in the case of both these techniques, meditation on point A and B, the time is limited to ten minutes. Both are available for men and women, point A with a certain change in the technique for women only, but otherwise there is no difference.

These two meditations on points A and B are very useful in correcting the disturbed tendencies of the mind. Since this tendency exists in the majority of cases these meditations can be safely advised to almost all abhyasis without exception.[2]

(p.131)

See, this is the logic of the spiritual journey. Whichever way I go the possibility of suffering is there, at least what I think of as suffering. So let me suffer going on rather than suffer going back. This is the only logic for the suffering that we seem to apparently have to expose ourselves to in Sahaj Marg. It is a pity that most people exaggerate their sufferings when they come into the system, and imagine that they are suffering more. Is it samskara? Is it cleaning? (p.185)

---

[2] Same instruction as for meditation on point A.

Have faith in the Master. Refer to him whenever you are in trouble. Meditate. It will give you all the answers that you need. When in trouble, clean yourselves. Even if you have a momentary spasm of anger against somebody or even against the Master, sit down and do a little cleaning. At that moment if you do the cleaning, it goes. (p.187)

As I said last time, the minimum effect will always be there. Thanks to the work of the Master, thanks to the capacity of the transmission, thanks to the effectiveness of the cleaning process, they cannot fail under any circumstance. (p.198)

If you want faithful abhyasis, you must be first faithful — full of faith. And to create it is our sadhana. I believe that all our system of cleaning and meditation and constant remembrance — these practices are tailor-made to precisely inject into us these qualities. (p.218)

Neither outside in the world of physics nor inside in the human heart can we find the Ultimate, except with the Master's help, who has to put it there for us. That is why we have this first sitting, where we clean the abhyasi, second sitting if necessary, third if necessary, fifth if necessary, seventeenth if necessary; and then when the cleaning is complete, we transmit; and as Babuji used to say, the lamp is lit inside. In that sense, to say that everything is divine is a travesty of the truth. It can be divine, but it **is** not divine.

You are actually infusing the divine into the heart of the abhyasi with the first transmission you give him, which must be after sufficient cleaning to receive that divine presence. (p.234-235)

When we start meditating, and if you are serious about it, and if you go about it properly, you must achieve this separation of the real self, the inner self, from this mundane self, which is but a machine run through the five senses under the control of the mind with an intellect supposed to guide it. This is precisely why people are not able to change, because the will is lacking. The intention is there, but until the samskaras are cleared off, for which you need an external agency to help you, there in no chance of an individual ever changing his or her life — be assured of this — the chances are absolutely zero.

That is why in spiritual life we have also to develop a certain amount of compassion, that if people are not changing it is not because they don't want to change but because they are unable to change. And this is important work that preceptors are supposed to do, you see, clean them, eradicate progressively the samskaras, so that the power of the past, the enormous potency of the past, wound up into the samskaric spring can be removed. Then the person becomes free, relatively speaking.   (p.246-247)

Preceptor's work has three elements: the first, the most important, and that which accounts for ninety percent of their work: **CLEANING**, Master has said that is the most important; and this is something we have to do all our lives; it never stops. Some people say after one cleaning, the work is over, but it is never over. So it is a general rule that when you give one sitting, say for thirty minutes, at least twenty minutes are devoted to cleaning.
(p.271)

Now, how to take a new abhyasi: it is the same principle; during the first two or three sittings, only cleaning, because if you transmit without cleaning, his tendencies will be strengthened. So, first purification, then transmission. Now everybody says we give a beginner two sittings or three sittings, but Master said in one case he gave 22 sittings! So it depends on how well we are able to see the condition and clean it. But as a general rule, it is three sittings minimum for commencement. And generally, they should be on three different days.　　　　　　　　　　　(p.272)

Q: How do we do the cleaning?

PR: By will-power.

Q: I thought cleaning was done with the transmission?

PR: It is not with the transmission. It is a great difference. It is very specific, Master's instructions.

...Q: An abhyasi who has had the three sittings but who did not come back for one year or two, do you have to start all over again?

PR: Well, it is not always necessary to start all over again, but it will be, in most cases, it will be necessary because of the condition. So you need to do the cleaning. So this is the mecha-nics of the preceptor's work.　　　　　　　　　　　(p.273)

Q: For cleaning, are there indications on sitting being terminated?

PR: The cleaning for each sitting can be complete; but it is not complete absolutely. You know, like when you have a bath. For that bath, it is sufficient; but again, you need a bath tomorrow.
　　　　　　　　　　　(p.274)

Q: And what about cleaning the atmosphere?

PR: It is better that you first learn the job with abhyasis. Because, if you do the work properly, the atmosphere will automatically be cleaned. Because that affects the atmosphere too! You know, **we** are spoiling the atmosphere. The original atmosphere is good. Master has written in *Reality at Dawn*, "By our thoughts, we have spoilt the atmosphere." So, when you clean the human hearts and their thoughts get purified, actions get purified, then the atmosphere gets purified too. That is how children benefit if the parents are abhyasis. Because in a natural way, they receive.

Q: Does the preceptor himself get cleaned?

PR: No. The preceptor has to do his own cleaning. But if you are so busy you don't have time for meditation, cleaning, then the Master will take care of you. But only if you are so busy! (p.276)

Q: What about cleaning yourself before giving a sitting?

PR- In groups, well in big groups, we rarely do much cleaning. You may do it for a few minutes. You see, generally, in mornings like Sunday morning, it is always transmission. But the Master advised, in the later years of his life, that a preceptor should do a few minutes cleaning for himself first, before transmitting. This can be done even while you are sitting in front of a group. You see, 7:30 is meditation. You sit at 7:25, and sit quietly for five minutes and do your own cleaning. It improves the quality of the whole sitting. This was not originally in the instructions.

Q: This should be only for group satsangh, not for individual?

PR: You see, you are not going to clean yourself before each sitting. It is not like a surgeon who washes his hands before every operation. In the morning, when you give your first transmission, at that time, yes.

Like Sunday group sitting, or Wednesday evening, like that, few minutes, two, three minutes, cleaning, then do transmission. But when you have a large group, it is basically transmission. You see, in individual sitting, the basic job is cleaning. It is not so much the transmission. In group sittings, it is more the transmission than cleaning. (p.276)

PR: It is largely the preceptor's work to determine who needs a cleaning.

Q: What are the indications of that need?

PR- You have to study the condition. You must be able to see so many people and say, "I want to give you a sitting tomorrow. You must call." But we have the contrary phenomena, that the abhyasis want to ask for individual sittings. What happens, you see, the abhyasi with a lot of interest, he is also comparatively cleaner than the other persons, but he keeps coming again and again. The other man who needs the sittings he never comes. And you must see that each abhyasi receives at least one individual sitting in a month, two per month would be better — once a fort-night.   (p.279)

Q: Why should yawning come when a preceptor is cleaning?

PR: Yawning does not come to all. It comes to some. One reason is, he may have eaten too much. The other reason is he may be feeling sleepy. Very rarely it is a spiritual reason. It is not during, it is after the cleaning. After a deep sitting, you will feel yawning, because during the sitting you get relaxation. Total relaxation.
                                                                              (p.281)

You see, what happens in the beginning is this. People are so gross, that from the higher regions, the grossness comes down to the heart. It is like cleaning a tank. The dirt is always settling on the bottom. The sides may be also dirty, but they are easily cleaned. Then you clean the bottom, put some more water, brush it again and finally the tap itself has to be cleaned. The dirty wa-ter comes out and then you fill fresh water, flush it out! So it is by gravity, you know! There seems to be a spiritual gravity like the physical gravity, and everything comes down over there.
                                                                              (p.286)

Q: How long should the cleaning be? When you give appointments to people and say you take one every half an hour, then when you feel an abhyasi has such a work that you go beyond the time, it will be more than half an hour.

PR: It is better to do one job well than to do six jobs incomplete. You see, time is only approximate. It is possible in other things, but not in spirituality. (p.287)

We have to concern ourselves with the solid work of cleaning the abhyasis, which should normally form at least eighty percent of our work — as was told by Babuji time and again. But as Master himself used to say, "Cleaning is the most essential part of the work." But it is difficult and time-consuming. (p.299)

A very common misconception is that cleaning is effected by transmission. If one reads through Master's instructions, he says, "Transmit for a few minutes, and try to read the condition of the abhyasi. Do this for four or five minutes. Then clean thoroughly. Then transmit again for a few minutes and read the condition again. If the cleaning is over, then transmit for the rest of the sitting." What is used in cleaning the abhyasi? It is the will power of the preceptor. Transmission is **stopped** when the cleaning is being done. Otherwise would not the transmission itself serve to exaggerate the latent tendencies of the individual? (p.299-300)

The idea that the abhyasi is to be cleaned to your satisfaction is also to be avoided. We work for the benefit of the abhyasis — not for our satisfaction. The two appear to be inter-linked, but the satisfaction should arise as a result of seeing the abhyasi's condition glowing. That is, he is to be put before the self. There is generally a limit to the extent of work that can be done in one sitting.

When this limit is reached the sitting comes to a natural conclusion. A perceptive preceptor perceives this, and brings the sitting to an end. Can you clean a really dirty towel in one wash? Sometimes it has to go through the cleaning process many times. Even an ink stain cannot be washed out in one wash, even when the stain is yet wet. The human grossness is so hard and densified, having been accumulated and compacted over millennia. How then can it be removed in one sitting, or even in one hundred? Do you see the magnitude of the work? (p.301)

I would suggest that as the cleaning proceeds, and as grossness is progressively removed, subtleness sets in as a consequence of the cleaning process. Unfortunately the effects are not perceived. Why? Because by the way of life that the abhyasis lead, they may be acquiring fresh grossness, so that the effect of the cleaning process gets vitiated. But if the abhyasi co-operates, and leads life in such a way that no fresh impressions are formed, then the possibility opens up for grossness to be progressively reduced — that is, he gets subtler and subtler. (p.303-304)

A Preceptor's Guide, Volume III
Shri P. Rajagopalachari

...character formation, for two reasons, is our business. One, because except for the rudimentary base we bring with us from the past life as a samskara, all the rest is the creation of the ego, which means ourselves — small. So when we have created, we have to work upon ourselves to destroy it.

The second is: not being part of the samskaric pattern, it is not really amenable to removal by the cleaning process. That is why you find there is a peculiar, what shall I say, confusion that people are being cleaned, they receive transmission, the inner change is going on, but outwardly there is no transformation. So our friends don't accept Sahaj Marg. Our relations don't accept Sahaj Marg. Society does not accept. It is all right for Babuji to say that if you look inside you will find there is almost a saint, but they say, "What of the outside? Why is there no change? Should there not be a change outside patterned on the change within?" (p.41-42)

It is no use being a saint inside, and a susceptible fellow outside. We are susceptible precisely because the behaviour is the same, and it responds to the environment in the same way. What happens is that you are reinforcing the samskaras which are being cleaned away by the Master in his immense humility and generosity, kindness, love for us, and his problem becomes perhaps eternal, insoluble. He goes on cleaning, we go on adding, not out of choice but out of a senseless repetition of the same behaviour because we have not bothered to change our personalities. (p.46)

I have told you this before when people weep. For heaven's sake, don't start hugging them and kissing them in the European manner, and lulling them into some sort of false security. Let them weep. It is one of the great cathartic devices, that nature gives us, you see. Let them weep, you see. Don't attend to them. Just you sit back calm, let them weep. When it is finished you say, "Now sit. Let us have a meditation." Remember when they weep like that it is the heart's way of making a silent confession, a confession which they cannot voice, which they cannot put into words. Perhaps guilt, perhaps shame, perhaps compounded of both. Let them weep. It is a cleaning, you see, that nature does from inside and we should not interfere with that process. (p.95)

... you would not plant the giant California redwood in the deserts of Africa. How do you expect it to come up? You would not put the fish that you take out, the most beautiful fish, and put it in ice on top of the Himalayas. The environment has to be prepared, therefore we have so much cleaning to do — upon ourselves as abhyasis, we are eternally abhyasis, upon others who come to us as abhyasis. And when we neglect this cleaning, either individual cleaning as abhyasis, or as preceptors working upon others, we are failing in our duty to prepare the soil into which the seed has been sown.   (p.123)

Proceedings of the Preceptors' Seminar
May 2 to 4, 1991, Pune, India
Shri P. Rajagopalachari

And then progressively the inner condition which is also eternal, the inner presence which is also eternal, begins to be revealed. We may marvel, we may wonder, but we should not become self-congratulatory and say, "Ah ha! I have done this," because we have really done nothing. It's like a man polishing the mirror to remove the dust from it, and then saying I have created a mirror. The mirror was already there, you have brushed off the dust.

So in that sense we are cleaners. Babuji Maharaj said, "I am the sweeper, I enter the gutters of humanity and clean them." Now there should be no revulsion, no pain because a gutter after all carries only our refuse, it is not something created by somebody else. It is our refuse that gutters carry. It is our refuse that these modern cars and wagons carry off from your houses, in beautiful black plastic bags. You see this tendency to hide rubbish is a very occidental tendency. It shows an inability to face facts. It shows a desire or a fear (chuckles) of looking at the dirty side of things. That is, we are trying to concentrate on one pole forgetting that the other pole also exists. It shows a revulsion of facts of life which are created by us.

When there is a mat of fallen dead leaves on the floor of a jungle, you don't say this is rubbish. It makes a nice cushion to sit upon. But when it is human offal, human excreta, or cow dung we, you know, perk up our noses in revulsion, as if it is some stink which is not created by us, but as if it is there and we want somebody to clean it away. See, this tendency to be revolted by one side of life prevents us from really appreciating the other aspect of life. We have a saying in Tamil that only one who has been in the sun can really enjoy the shade. If you are in the shade all the time you do not know the value of that shade.   (p.15-16)

Failure is a stepping stone to success more than anywhere else in spiritual work because the more we fail, the more we think of the Master, the more we bring his presence into the picture, and say, "Master, please come to my help." Later on we say, "Master, please." No come to my help because who am I that I should be given the help? It is the abhyasi who is to be helped. Why should he help me to do my work which is His work I'm doing? I mean if he is to give me the work and then come to my aid every time I sit to clean somebody, isn't it ridiculous? That Master should sack the preceptor concerned immediately.   (p.17)

Often I have been told by Babuji, "You don't have to sit in meditation, you don't have to do anything. You carry on with the work that is given to you." "But Babuji, group sitting, I miss all those wonderful experiences, sublime experiences, going into samadhi." "Not for you." Remember what Babuji said, "A saint is not for his own enjoyment but is to be enjoyed by others." A preceptor doesn't work for his own evolution or her own evolution but for the evolution of others. A preceptor may live under very dirty circumstances in his house but if he keeps the houses of others clean, he is a good preceptor.

When your house is unclean, dirty, because you have no time to do it, to clean it, because you are involved in other people's work, there is no shame, there is no harm, there is no blame. But if it is filthy because you are indolent and lazy and lie abed until nine o'clock in the morning, eleven o'clock in the morning, that is a crime. It is breaking the first maxim of our ten maxims.   (p.18)

So you see, the difficulty here is to keep a person alive by not killing him. Dosage being most important, cleaning being extremely important because one without the other is an unbalanced treatment. A clean person receives more and more, whereas one who is gross if you transmit too much the grossness is increased, the tendencies are more developed in that direction. Again and again we have said that, "If you transmit to a crook, he will become a perfect crook in time."   (p.23)

Babuji has said, "A saint is for the enjoyment of the world." Without the world what will a saint do? But that doesn't mean we have to be sinners so that there can be a saint to redeem us. We should not make ourselves dirty so that he can clean us, and so we can prove the efficacy of the system. "No, no, you see, I am the grossest and yet it has worked. I went and acquired grossness especially to prove Ram Chandraji's cleaning method." It might fail!   (p.299)

So all these technicalities of practice, the technology of Sahaj Marg, the principles, the maxims, of course we need them, but I would like to see a day coming when they cease to exist. Not because of lack of reverence for my Master, or for the teaching that he has created, but that was what he himself would have wished. When it is no longer to tell abhyasis, "Every morning you must sit in meditation, every evening you must do the cleaning, I am telling you," then there is a perfect society, there is a perfect society of meditators, spiritual aspirants, who now have a right to say, "I have a Master. I am practising a method and there is a Mission which propagates it." (p.314)

Down Memory Lane, Volume I
Shri P. Rajagopalachari

The first hurdle in life is the completion of one's first year of terrestrial existence. Therefore when a baby completes the age of one, there is a religious ceremony of cleansing and propitiation. The child's horoscope is not cast till it completes the first year!
(p.163)

Glossary

ANUBHAV: Intuitional perception or personal experience in the realm of Nature or God.

ATMA CHAKRA: Heart chakra. In Sahaj Marg, the second, or soul, point.

ATMAN: Soul

BHOG (or BHOGA): Process of undergoing effects of impressions; experience; enjoyment.

BRAHMAND MANDAL: Mental sphere, supra-material sphere, cosmic region; sphere where everything manifests under a subtle shape before taking place in the material world.

BHUTA SUDDHI: Cleansing of the soul.

CHAKRA: Centre of super-vital forces located in different parts of the body; figuratively called lotus.

COCHON: French word meaning 'pig'.

DARSHAN: Vision of someone's inner reality.

DHRUVA (DHRUV PAD): Highly evolved soul. First or lowest level of cosmic functionary. Below the Dhruvadhipati.

DHRUVAGATI: State of Dhruva.

HANUMAN: Monkey servant of Lord Rama.

HATHA YOGA: The first four steps of Patanjali's Ashtanga Yoga. The practice of yoga concerning the physical body.

INDRIYAS: Ten senses/organs of Indian philosophy, subdivided as *gyana* and *karma* indriyas. The former are five senses pertaining to perception, knowledge or wisdom, while the latter are five senses pertaining mainly to action.

JEEVAN MUKTI (also JIVAN MOKSHA): Liberation while one is still living, or more precisely, incarnated in a human body.

KANTHA CHAKRA: Throat plexus (vishuddha chakra).

KRIYA: Action

LAYAWASTHA (or LAYAVASTHA): The state of mergence.

MAHARAJ: Literally supreme king, used as a title for a great person.

MANAS: Psyche, mind.

MARG: Way, path.

MUNI: See RISHI.

NABHI: Navel.

NETI-NETI: The principle of 'not this, not this'.

PANCHA: Five.

PINDA PRADESH: Material sphere; the heart region.

PRANAHUTI: Process of yogic transmission; derived from *prana* meaning life and *ahuti* meaning offering. Offering of life force by the guru into the disciple's heart.

PRARABDHA: Fate, destiny.

PRECEPTOR: An abhyasi prepared and permitted by the Master to impart spiritual training through the utilization of *pranahuti* or yogic transmission.

PUJA: A physical ritualistic act of worshipping a deity (in Sahaj Marg, the meditation practice).

RAJA YOGA (or RAJ YOGA): Ancient system or science followed by the great rishis and saints which helped them to realise the Self or God. Usually used for meditative practices, as distinguished from hatha yoga.

RAND: South African currency.

RISHI: Saint; seer; one who has realised Self (usually through meditative practices).

SADHAK: Disciple who practises a sadhana.

SADHANA: Spiritual practice.

SAHAJ MARG: Natural path, simple path.

SAMADHI: The eighth and final step of Patanjali's Ashtanga Yoga; original balance. State in which we stay attached to Reality. In Sahaj Marg, the return to the original condition, which reigned in the beginning.

Babuji split the word into *sama*, meaning balance, and *adhi*, meaning original or ancient.

SAMARTH GURU (or SAMARTHA GURU): A perfect guru, who possesses all the qualities. A perfectly balanced guru.

SAMSKARAS (or SANSKARAS): Impressions. In Sahaj Marg, considered to be obstacles for spiritual progress.

SANDHYAVANDANA KRIYA: Evening prayer procedure.

SANKALPA: A subtle idea; an act of will.

SANSKRIT: Culture; also name of the ancient language of India.

SANSTHA: Spiritual tradition; organization; group.

SAPTALOKA: All the seven worlds.

SATSANGH (or SATSANG): 1. Spiritual assembly; 2. Being with Reality.

SHAKTI: Power.

SHASTRAS: Holy books (scriptures).

SITTING: A session of meditation, usually lasting from thirty minutes to an hour, in which the Master or a preceptor meditates with a group or an individual for the purpose of cleaning and transmission.

SOOKSHMA SHARIR: Astral body, subtle body.

VAIRAGYA: Renunciation, detachment.

VASANAS: Past impressions

VASU: Another name for Krishna. Also refers to cosmic functionary below the Dhruva, an elevated person who performs the lowest level of godly work entrusted to him.

YAMA: The first step of Patanjali's Ashtanga Yoga. Refers to the purity of body and mind. Also, Lord of Death.

YATRA: Voyage; journey; pilgrimage; the inner spiritual process.

YOGA: Literally meaning the unity of the soul with the supreme soul. Also acceptable to mean practices that lead to the state of oneness.

YOGI: One who practises yoga; one who achieves union with the Absolute.

References

SHRI RAM CHANDRA OF FATEHGARH, U.P.

Truth Eternal, 3rd ed., Shri Ram Chandra Mission, Shahjahanpur, India, 1987.

SHRI RAM CHANDRA OF SHAHJAHANPUR, U.P.

Complete Works of Ram Chandra, vol. I, Shri Ram Chandra Mission, North American Publishing Committee, Pacific Grove, CA, USA, 1989.

————, vol. II, Shri Ram Chandra Mission, North American Publishing Committee, Pacific Grove, CA, USA, 1991.

————, vol. III, Shri Ram Chandra Mission, USA, 1997.

Letters of the Master, vol. I, ed. by Thomas J. Whitlam, Shri Ram Chandra Mission, North American Publishing Committee, Pacific Grove, CA, USA, 1992.

————, vol. II, ed. by Thomas J. Whitlam, Shri Ram Chandra Mission, North American Publishing Committee, Pacific Grove, CA, USA, 1992.

————, vol. III, ed. by Shri Rajendrasinh N. Rathod, Shri Ram Chandra Mission, North American Publishing Committee, Molena, GA, USA, 1996.

SHRI PARTHASARATHI RAJAGOPALACHARI

Blossoms in the East, Shri Ram Chandra Mission, Shahjahanpur, India, 1977.

Down Memory Lane, vol. I, Shri Ram Chandra Mission, North American Publishing Committee, Pacific Grove, CA, USA, 1993.

The Fruit of the Tree, Shri Ram Chandra Mission, Shahjahanpur, India, 1988.

The Garden of Hearts, Shri Ram Chandra Mission, Shahjahanpur, India, 1980.

Heart of the Lion, Shri Ram Chandra Mission, North American Publishing Committee, Pacific Grove, CA, USA, 1993.

Heart to Heart, vol. I, Shri Ram Chandra Mission, Shahjahanpur, India, 1988.

——————, vol. II, Shri Ram Chandra Mission, North American Publishing Committee, Pacific Grove, CA, USA, 1991.

——————, vol. III, Shri Ram Chandra Mission, North American Publishing Committee, Pacific Grove, CA, USA, 1994.

India in the West, Shri Ram Chandra Mission, Shahjahanpur, India, 1973.

In His Footsteps, vol. I, Shri Ram Chandra Mission, North American Publishing Committee, Pacific Grove, CA, USA, 1988.

——————, vol. II, Shri Ram Chandra Mission, North American Publishing Committee, Pacific Grove, CA, USA, 1993.

——————, vol. III, Shri Ram Chandra Mission, North American Publishing Committee, Molena, GA, USA, 1995.

Love and Death, Shri Ram Chandra Mission, North American Publishing Committee, Pacific Grove, CA, USA, 1992.

My Master, 6th ed., Shri Ram Chandra Mission, Shahjahanpur, India, 1989.

A Preceptor's Guide, vol. II, Shri Ram Chandra Mission, North American Publishing Committee, Pacific Grove, CA, USA, 1990.

——————, vol. III, Shri Ram Chandra Mission, North American Publishing Committee, Pacific Grove, CA, USA, 1990.

The Principles of Sahaj Marg, vol. I, Shri Ram Chandra Mission, Shahjahanpur, India, 1986.

——————, vol. II, Shri Ram Chandra Mission, Shahjahanpur, India, 1987.

——————, vol. III, Shri Ram Chandra Mission, Shahjahanpur, India, 1987.

——————, vol. IV, Shri Ram Chandra Mission, Shahjahanpur, India, 1988.

——————, vol. V, Shri Ram Chandra Mission, Shahjahanpur, India, 1989.

——————, vol. VI, Shri Ram Chandra Mission, Shahjahanpur, India, 1990.

——————, vol.VII, Shri Ram Chandra Mission, Shahjahanpur, India, 1993.

————, vol.VIII, Shri Ram Chandra Mission, Shahjahanpur, India, 1994.

————, vol.IX, Shri Ram Chandra Mission, Shahjahanpur, India, 1995.

————, vol.X, Shri Ram Chandra Mission, Shahjahanpur, India, 1997.

Proceedings of the Preceptors' Seminar, Shri Ram Chandra Mission, Shahjahanpur, India, 1992. (No significant quotations on meditation have been selected.)

Proceedings of the Seminar on Sahaj Marg (Vorauf — Munich, Germany), Shri Ram Chandra Mission, Germany, 1985.

Religion and Spirituality, Shri Ram Chandra Mission, North American Publishing Committee, Pacific Grove, CA, USA, 1992.

Revealing the Personality, Shri Ram Chandra Mission, Denmark, 1992.

Role of the Master in Human Evolution, Shri Ram Chandra Mission, Munich, West Germany, 1986.

Sahaj Marg in Europe, Shri Ram Chandra Mission, Shahjahanpur, India, 1976.

What Is Sahaj Marg? — A Preceptor's Guide, vol. I, Shri Ram Chandra Mission, North American Publishing Committee, Pacific Grove, CA, USA, 1988.

This is only a partial listing of Sahaj Marg publications. For a complete listing, please write to:

Shri Ram Chandra Mission
Post Office Box 269
Molena, GA 30258 USA